I thoroughly enjoyed this book! I'm convinced that laughter is absolutely the best medicine as it charges the immune system and triggers the relaxation response. In this stressful world where 75 to 90 percent of all visits to primary care physicians are for stress-related complaints or disorders, I believe *Laugh Yourself Healthy* is a vital part of the healing process. Laughter stops stress in its tracks. Charles and Frances Hunter have put together a wonderful collection of humorous anecdotes to help brighten your day and your disposition. After all, "a merry heart doeth good like medicine."

—Don Colbert, MD
New York Times Best-selling Author of
The Seven Pillars of Health and the Bible Cure series

Charles and Frances are very special, longtime friends of mine. Through the years, they have always been so encouraging and full of the joy of the Lord. I know that as you read *Laugh Yourself Healthy* you will receive that joy and be strengthened and encouraged, experiencing God's healing in every area of your life!

—Joel Osteen
Senior Pastor, Lakewood Church
Houston, TX

P9-DYD-583

Laugh
Yourself
Healthy

Charles & Frances
HUNTER

Christian
LIFE
A STRANG COMPANY

Most STRANG COMMUNICATIONS BOOK GROUP products are available at special quantity discounts for bulk purchase for sales promotions, premiums, fundraising, and educational needs. For details, write Strang Communications Book Group, 600 Rinehart Road, Lake Mary, Florida 32746, or telephone (407) 333-0600.

LAUGH YOURSELF HEALTHY by Charles and Frances Hunter
Published by Christian Life
A Strang Company
600 Rinehart Road
Lake Mary, Florida 32746
www.strangbookgroup.com

Unless otherwise noted, Scripture quotations are from the King James Version of the Bible.

Design Director: Bill Johnson; Cover design by Amanda Potter

Our very special thanks to Roger Wolfe, publisher of *The Tulsa Morning Fax*, from which most of these jokes were taken, for his permission to use them in this book.

Library of Congress Cataloging-in-Publication Data:
Hunter, Charles, 1920-
  Laugh yourself healthy / Charles and Frances Hunter.
    p. cm.
  Previously pub.: Healing through humor. Lake Mary, Fla. : Creation House Press, c2003.
  ISBN-13: 978-1-59979-349-8
  ISBN-10: 1-59185-196-3
  1. American wit and humor. I. Hunter, Frances Gardner, 1916- II. Title.

  PN6165.H93 2008
  818'.602--dc22
                                    2008014811
Previously published as *Healing Through Humor* by Creation House, copyright © 2003, ISBN: 978-1-59185-196-7.

09 10 11 12 13 — 9 8 7 6 5 4 3
Printed in the United States of America

CONTENTS

Foreword by Francisco Contreras, MD vii

Anatomy of a Laugh ix

Preface xi

1   Mind Twisters 1

2   Love and Marriage 17

3   Chuckle With Children 29

4   Parenting Predicaments 40

5   Short and to the Point 45

6   Joke Theology 101 56

7   Nutritional Humor 74

8   Our Four-Legged Friends 95

9   Lighthearted Aging 106

10   Purse String Musings 122

11   Smiling at the Law 132

12   Living Life With a Smile 150

FOREWORD

I REMEMBER THOROUGHLY ENJOYING Robin Williams's portrayal of the young Dr. Patch Adams, a physician who spends more time in clown's garb than a doctor's gown. *Patch Adams,* the movie, brought to the world's attention the importance of compassion, love, and humor in the treatment of patients. My soul resonated with the message that joy is vital to the recuperation of health.

I could relate to the theme profoundly because I had grown up in and around the Oasis of Hope Hospital, which my dad founded in 1963 with the mission of improving the quality of the physical, emotional, and spiritual lives of his patients. His total-care approach included ministering to the patients' bodies with nutrition, nutraceuticals, pharmaceuticals, and physical therapy. It also involved nurturing the emotional and spiritual needs of his patients through counseling, music therapy, art therapy, prayer, hugs, and laughter. It came as no shock to me when my father pulled out his pen pal file full of the letters he had exchanged with the real Patch Adams since the early 1980s.

Dad and Patch are two birds of a feather. When I had the pleasure of spending time with Patch, I saw that holistic healing was no joking matter to him. He was dead serious. If you saw the movie and wondered if Patch is the same in real life, the answer is—the movie presented a tame version. The depth of Patch's knowledge and his commitment to humanity awed me. I was surprised to see that his doctor's bag was full of different clown noses and teeth, which he allowed me to try on, causing us both to laugh.

My father is the only physician I have met who would arrive at the hospital toting a guitar and a joke book. His career spanned sixty years. He was recognized with the Alternative Medicine Lifetime Achievement Award, but his biggest reward was that each day he could build a meaningful, healing relationship with his patients. I believe that not only was the laughter with patients healing for them, but it was also the key to the longevity of his career. One clinical study indicated that both patient *and* physician benefit from sessions of laughter. I don't doubt that to be true.

I have often said that fear is the stronghold of cancer. Cancer is an opportunistic disease. Fear and other negative emotions are detrimental to the immune system. Depression and anxiety are open invitations for cancer to have its way with a patient. When we are able to help a person smile and laugh, I know that we increase the possibility of recovery markedly. One of my goals is to help patients get to a place where they can stare cancer right in the eyes and say, "You cannot rob my joy." For me, laughter therapy is not a warm fuzzy activity that is a nice service to offer patients if time allows. It is an essential part of our treatment program.

Science has definitively confirmed the potent healing factor of laughter. Whether studies were conducted in Japan[1] or Loma Linda, California,[2] objective results indicate that patients who experience laughter receive a boost to their immune system as measured in the elevation of natural killer cell activity and immunoglobulin. There are so many objective clinical trials that support the healing power of humor that it surprises me that few doctors take advantage of this medication. I do realize that insurance companies probably do not reimburse doctors for telling jokes, but who cares? As physicians, we should be willing to do whatever it takes to improve the health of our patients.

This wonderful book, *Laugh Yourself Healthy*, is a great tool for doctors to use in laughter therapy sessions. As I mentioned, my father always brought a book of jokes with him to work. I think this book would have been one of his all-time favorites because it will keep any reader in stitches. I know that we are living in a time when everyone is panicked about medical claims and lawsuits, so I will make no claim about the healing power of this book. All I will say is that science confirms that positive emotions invoked by humor have healing effects. If you read this book and no positive emotions come about, you need to check if you have a pulse. This book is great, and I plan to prescribe it to my patients! Enjoy.

—Francisco Contreras, MD
Surgical Oncologist
Author, *The Coming Cancer Cure*
Director, Oasis of Hope Hospital
www.oasisofhope.com

---

1. K. Takahashi et al., "The Elevation of Natural Killer Cell Activity Induced by Laughter in a Crossover Study," *International Journal of Molecular Medicine* 8, no. 6 (December 2001): 645–650.
2. L. S. Berk et al., "Modulation of Neuroimmune Parameters During the Eustress or Humor-Associated Mirthful Laughter," *Alternative Therapies in Health and Medicine* 7, no 2 (March 2001): 62–72, 74–76.

ANATOMY OF A LAUGH

Your WHOLE BODY gets a kick out of a good chuckle. Here is what happens when you laugh, according to research.

- Your heart and lungs are stimulated.

- Your heart beats faster and your blood pressure rises temporarily.

- You breathe deeper and oxygenate more blood.

- Your body releases endorphins, your own natural pain-killers, and you produce more immune cells.

- You burn seventy-eight times as many calories as you would in a resting state.

- Your diaphragm, facial muscles, and internal organs all get bounced around in what is sometimes called "internal jogging."

After you've laughed, your muscles and arteries relax. That's great for easing pain. Also, your blood pressure lowers and your pulse drops below normal. Some researchers think all this aids digestion.

A merry heart doeth good like a medicine: but a broken spirit drieth the bones.
—Proverbs 17:22

A merry heart maketh a cheerful countenance: but by sorrow of the heart the spirit is broken.
—Proverbs 15:13

PREFACE

WRITE A BOOK called *Healing Through Humor!*" This is what the Lord told us to do. Of the fifty-four books we have written, none of them contain a joke; so we didn't think we were qualified. But when God tells you to do something, He will qualify you!

For months we researched thousands and thousands and thousands of jokes and selected the ones that we felt were the greatest immune builders.

Now, why did God tell us to write a book like that?

One night we were privileged to hear Dr. Francisco Contreras on TBN. His father was the founder of the great cancer research hospital in Tijuana, Mexico. We had visited there when we were in Tijuana several years ago and were tremendously impressed because the entire operation is bathed in prayer. So I listened very closely to what Dr. Contreras said.

Somewhere in the interview he made a statement that caused bells to ring in my head! He said, "One bout of anger will diminish the efficiency of your immune system for six hours, but one good laugh will increase the efficiency of your immune system for twenty-four hours." The immune system is what controls how healthy or how sick we are, so we all want to keep our immune systems as powerful as we can!

READ SLOWLY

Remember that when you squeeze an orange, you squeeze it and squeeze it until you get all the juice out of it. This joke book is meant to be read in exactly the same way. Don't read this book quickly or just scan it. You need to get all the juice out of each joke, so meditate on each joke until the humor has really hit you hard.

This is meant to be a book for you to just pick up, open anywhere in the book, and get a good laugh to increase your immune system. We would suggest that you read no more than five pages at a time.

Remember that the joy of the Lord is your strength, and a broken spirit dries your bones. Have a good laugh, and get your immune system going right now!

—Charles and Frances Hunter

one

MIND TWISTERS

Mental test

"Would you mind telling me, Doctor," Bob asked, "how you detect a mental deficiency in somebody who appears completely normal?"

"Nothing is easier," he replied. "You ask him a simple question that everyone should answer with no trouble. If he hesitates, that puts you on the track."

"What sort of question?"

"Well, you might ask him, 'Captain Cook made three trips around the world and died during one of them. Which one?'"

Bob thought for a moment and then said with a nervous laugh, "You wouldn't happen to have another example, would you? I don't know much about history."

A man came home from the psychiatrist with great news for his wife. "Honey, the doctor no longer has to treat me. He doesn't think I have an inferiority complex. He thinks I'm just inferior."

An airline captain was breaking in a very pretty, new stewardess. The route they were flying had an overnight stay in another city, so upon their arrival, the captain showed the blonde stewardess the best place for airline personnel to eat, shop, and stay overnight.

The next morning, as the pilot was preparing the crew for the day's route, he noticed that the new stewardess was missing. He knew which room she was in at the hotel and called her up, wondering what happened to her.

She answered the phone sobbing and said she couldn't get out of her room.

The captain was puzzled until she explained that her room had only three doors: one was to the bathroom, another led to the closet, and the third had a sign hanging on it that said, "Please Do Not Disturb!"

Things to think about

- How can batteries die?
- Why are buildings called buildings when they are finished? Shouldn't they be called builts?
- Would a fly without wings be called a walk?
- Can vegetarians eat animal crackers?

Did you know?

- It is impossible to lick your elbow.
- A shrimp's heart is in its head.
- People say, "Bless you," when you sneeze because when you sneeze, your heart stops for a millisecond.
- It is physically impossible for pigs to look up into the sky.
- No word in the English language rhymes with *month, orange, silver,* or *purple.*
- Did you hear about the man who couldn't call 911 because there was no 11 on the phone?

A university student was visiting relatives in Boston over the holidays. He went to a large party and met a pretty coed. He attempted to start up a conversation with the line, "Where does you go to school?"

The coed, of course, was not overly impressed with his grammar, but she did answer his question. "Yale," she said.

The university linebacker took a big, deep breath and shouted, "Where does you go to school?"

Wondering

Is it true that cannibals don't eat clowns because they taste funny?

Two inebriated men were riding on a roller coaster. One turned to the other and yelled, "Hey, we're really making great time, but I'm not sure this is the right bus!"

Asking the right question at the right time

A beautiful blonde was walking down the street and stopped a man to ask for the time.

The man, looking at his watch, helpfully responded, "Why certainly, miss. It's now four o'clock."

The blonde paused and said, "You know, it's really weird. I've been asking people that question all day long, and each time I get a different answer.

An important official who was visiting a mental institution made a telephone call but had difficulty getting his number. Finally, in exasperation he shouted to the operator, "Look here, girl, do you know who I am?"

"No," she replied calmly, "but I know where you are."

Applause, applause

Ten yuppettes and one elderly lady were hanging on to a rope that came down from a plane. They all decided that one person should get off because the combined weight of the people was too much for the rope. All of the people were afraid that the rope would soon break.

For a while no one spoke. Then the elderly lady said, "I've lived a good life. I'll let go." But before she did, the ten yuppettes started clapping.

I just bought a cured ham.
Wonder what it had?

A good question

Passing an office building late one night, Paula saw a sign that said, "Press bell for night watchman."

She did so, and after several minutes she heard the watchman clomping down the stairs. The uniformed man proceeded to unlock first one gate and then another, shut down the alarm system, and finally made his way through the revolving door.

"Well," he snarled at Paula, "what do you want?"

"I just wanted to know why you can't ring it for yourself."

Telling the truth

A woman was in a gambling casino for the first time. At the roulette table she said, "I have no idea what number to play."

A young, good-looking man nearby suggested that she play her age.

Smiling and blinking her eyelashes at the man, she put her money on number 32. The wheel was spun and 41 came up.

The smile drifted from the woman's face and she fainted.

From a passenger ship one can see a bearded man on a small island; he is shouting and desperately waving his hands.

"Who is it?" a passenger asks the captain.

"I have no idea. Every year when we pass, he goes mad."

A cup of coffee

Cousin Susie was the world's worst at getting instructions mixed up. So she decided to follow each and every instruction to the "T" on everything. That way she expected she wouldn't mess anything up.

When she got married, her husband bought her one of those fancy, electric coffee makers. It had all the latest gadgets on it.

Susie listened to Salesman Jones carefully explain how everything worked—how to plug it in, set the timer, go back to bed, and, upon rising, the coffee is ready.

A few weeks later, Susie was back in the store, and Jones asked her how she liked the coffee maker.

"Wonderful!" she replied. "However, there's one thing I don't understand. Why do I have to go back to bed every time I want a cup of coffee?"

Pumping iron

My grandfather worked in a blacksmith shop when he was a boy, and he used to tell me how he had toughened himself up so he could stand the rigors of blacksmithing.

He said he would stand outside the house and, with a five-pound potato sack in each hand, extend his arms straight out to his sides and hold them there as long as he could. He did this religiously for three weeks.

After a while he tried ten-pound potato sacks, then fifty-pound potato sacks, and finally he got to where he could lift a one-hundred-pound potato sack in each hand and hold his arms straight out for a full minute!

He never missed a day and performed this exercise in the hottest weather. He was determined to be the best blacksmith in the country.

Eventually, he started putting potatoes in the sacks.

Hopeless

"It's no good, sir," said the hopeless pupil to his English teacher. "I try to learn, but everything you say goes in both ears and out the other."

"Goes in both ears and out the other?" asked the puzzled teacher. "But you have only two ears, boy."

"You see, sir? I'm no good at math either."

Flight plans

On a plane bound for New York, the flight attendant approached a beautiful blonde sitting in the first class section and requested that she move to coach since she did not have a first class ticket. The blonde replied, "I'm young, I'm beautiful, I'm going to New York, and I'm not moving."

Not wanting to argue with a customer, the flight attendant asked the copilot to speak with her. He went to talk to the woman, asking her to please move out of the first class section.

Again, the blonde replied, "I'm young, I'm beautiful, I'm going to New York, and I'm not moving."

The copilot returned to the cockpit and asked the captain what he should do.

The captain went to the first class section and whispered in the lady's ear. She immediately jumped up and ran to the coach's section mumbling to herself, "Why didn't you just say so?"

Surprised, the flight attendant and the copilot asked what he said to her that finally convinced her to move from her seat.

He said, "I told her the first class section wasn't going to New York."

More flight plans

It was a young blonde's first plane trip. She boarded the aircraft and found her a window seat in the nonsmoking section and settled in.

A man came over and insisted that she was in his seat. She told him to go away.

"OK," replied the man. "If that's the way you want it, you fly the plane."

LOGIC 101

1. The Japanese eat very little fat and suffer fewer heart attacks than the British or Americans.
2. On the other hand, the French eat a lot of fat and also suffer fewer heart attacks than the British or Americans.
3. Conclusion: Eat what you like. It's speaking English that's killing you.

Logic quiz

"It's time to see how clearly you can think," the teacher said to his class. "Now, listen carefully, and think about what I'm saying. I'm thinking of a person who has the same mother and father as I have. But this person is not my brother or sister. Who is it?"

The kids in the class furrowed their brows, scratched their heads, and otherwise showed how hard they were thinking. But no one came up with the right answer.

When everyone in the class had given up, the teacher announced, "The person is me."

Little Jeffrey beamed at learning the answer. "That's a good one," he said to himself. "I'll have to try that on Mom and Dad while we're eating dinner tonight."

That night little Jeffrey repeated the riddle to his parents. "I'm thinking of a person who has the same mother and father that I have," he said. "But this person isn't my brother or sister. Who is it?"

His parents furrowed their brows, scratched their heads, and otherwise pretended they were thinking hard. After a while they both looked up at Jeffrey and said, "We give up. Who is it?"

"It's my teacher!" Jeffrey shouted.

How can you live without knowing these things?

- Every day more money is printed for Monopoly than for the U.S. Treasury.
- Coca-Cola was originally green.
- 111,111,111 x 111,111,111 = 12,345,678,987,654,321
- If a statue in the park of a person on a horse has both front legs in the air, the person died in battle. If the horse has one front leg in the air, the person died as a result of

wounds received in battle. If the horse has all four legs on the ground, the person died of natural causes.

- Hershey's Kisses are called that because the machine that makes them looks like it's kissing the conveyor belt.

Q: What do bulletproof vests, fire escapes, windshield wipers, and laser printers all have in common?

A: They were all invented by women.

Common sense

A monastery in Europe is perched high on a cliff several hundred feet in the air. The only way to reach the monastery is to be suspended in a basket, which is pulled to the top by several monks who pull and tug with all their strength. Obviously, one ride up the steep cliff is terrifying. One tourist got exceedingly nervous about halfway up as he noticed that the rope by which he was suspended was old and frayed. With a trembling voice he asked the monk who was riding with him in the basket how often they changed the rope.

The monk responded brusquely, "Whenever it breaks."

Mathematical puzzle

Think of a number.

Multiply it by 3.

Now add 5.

Take away the number you first thought of.

Now add 7.

Subtract 4.

Add back the number you first thought of.

Now close your eyes.

Dark, isn't it?

Correct pronunciation

A man and his wife were driving their RV across country and were nearing a town called Kissimmee. They noted the strange spelling and tried to figure out how to pronounce it—Kiss-a-me, Kis-sa-me, Kis-sa-mee. They grew more perplexed as they drove into town. Since they were hungry, they pulled into a place to get something to eat. At the counter, the man said to the waitress, "My wife and I can't seem to be able to figure out how to pronounce this place. Will you tell me where we are and say it very slowly so I can understand?"

The waitress looked at him and said, "Buuuurrrrrgerrr Kiiinnnng."

A cold winter coming

During the first part of autumn, the Indians asked their chief if the winter was going to be cold or mild. Not really knowing the answer, the chief replied that the winter was going to be very cold and that the members of the village were to collect wood to be prepared.

Being a good leader, he then called the National Weather Service and asked, "Is this winter going to be cold?"

The man on the phone responded, "Yes, this winter will be quite cold indeed."

Hearing that, the chief went back to speed up his people in their efforts of collecting wood so that they would be prepared for the coming season.

A week later he again called the National Weather Service and asked, "Is it going to be a cold winter?"

"Yes," the man replied, "it's going to be a very cold winter."

The chief went back to his people and ordered them to keep collecting wood.

Two weeks later he again called the National Weather Service to get evidence for their prediction. "On what do you predict such a cold winter?" he asked.

"Our evidence is indisputable," answered the meteorologist. "The Indians are collecting firewood like crazy!"

Following directions

Billy Joe came to work looking sheepish and embarrassed. His friend Jim finally pried the problem out of him. Billy Joe explained, "I received a party invitation for last night, and it plainly said, 'Black tie only.' But when I got there, everyone else was wearing suits too!"

Needing just a little sleep

A man had been driving all night and by morning was still far from his destination. He decided to stop at the next city he came to and park somewhere quiet so he could get an hour or two of sleep.

The quiet place he chose happened to be on one of the city's major jogging routes. No sooner had he settled back to snooze than there came a knocking on his window. He looked out and saw a jogger running in place.

"Excuse me, sir," the jogger said. "Do you have the time?"

The man looked at the car clock and answered, "8:15."

"Thanks," responded the jogger as he jogged off.

The man settled down again, and soon another jogger tapped on the window. "Excuse me, sir. Do you have the time?"

"8:25," answered the man.

The jogger said thanks as he left. Now the man could see other joggers passing by, and he knew it was only a matter of time before another one disturbed him.

To avoid the problem, he got out a pen and paper and put a sign in the window saying, "I do not know the time!"

Once again he settled back to sleep. He was just dozing off when there was another knock on the window.

"Sir! Sir! It's 8:45."

A student was asked if he knew what *Roe v. Wade* was about. He answered that he thought it was the decision George Washington had to make when he decided to cross the Delaware.

Groaner

A musician who joined an orchestra on a cruise ship was having a terrible time keeping time with the rest of the band. Finally, the bandleader said, "Look, either you learn to keep time, or I'll throw you overboard. It's up to you—sync or swim."

The secret of life

Mike and Ernie were constant companions. Mike was a calm, laid-back individual who never complained. Ernie was very nervous and a constant complainer. One day Ernie said to Mike, "Mike, how do you manage to get along with everyone?"

"Oh, I just never disagree with anybody."

"Mike, you're a liar!" exclaimed Ernie.

"I know it."

Get yo' momma

A family from the hills was visiting the city and was in a mall for the first time in their lives. The father and son were strolling around while the wife shopped.

They were amazed by almost everything they saw, but especially by two shiny, silver walls that could move apart and then slide back together again.

"Pa," asked the boy, "what's that?"

The father, never having seen an elevator, responded, "Son, I dunno. I ain't never seen anything like that in my entire life. I ain't got no idear."

While the boy and his father were watching in amazement, an old lady walked up to the moving walls and pressed a button.

The walls opened, and the lady walked between them into a small room. The walls closed, and the boy and his father watched the small circular numbers above the walls light up sequentially.

They continued to watch until it reached the last number, and then the numbers began to light up in reverse order. Then the walls opened up again, and a gorgeous, voluptuous woman who looked to be in her twenties stepped out.

The father, not taking his eyes off the young woman, said quietly to his son, "Boy, go git yo' momma!"

A man mentioned to his landlord about the tenants in the apartment over his apartment. "Many a night they stomp on the floor and shout until midnight."

When the landlord asked if it bothered him, he replied, "Not really. I usually stay up and practice my trumpet until about that time most every night anyway."

Just checking

The shipwrecked mariner had spent several years on a deserted island. Then one morning he was thrilled to see a ship offshore and a smaller vessel pulling out toward him. When the boat grounded on the beach, the officer in charge handed the marooned sailor a bundle of newspapers and told him, "With the captain's compliments. He said to read through these and let us know if you still want to be rescued."

Yuppette Jokes

Why did the yuppette stare at the can of frozen orange juice? Because it said *concentrate*.

Why do yuppettes always smile during lightning storms? They think their picture is being taken.

The yuppette and the truck driver

A yuppette had just gotten a new sports car and was out for a drive when she accidentally cut off a truck driver who had been driving for hours. He motioned her to pull over. When she did, he got out of the truck and pulled a piece of chalk from his pocket. He drew a circle on the side of the road and commanded the yuppette, "Stand in that circle and don't move!"

He opened her car doors and cut up her leather seats. When he turned around, she had a little grin on her face. Infuriated, he said, "Oh, you think that's funny? Watch this!"

He got a baseball bat out of his truck and broke every window in her car. When he turned and looked at her, she began to giggle. He was really mad now and proceeded to slash all her tires. Now she began laughing out loud.

The truck driver was really starting to lose it. He went to his truck and got a can of gas, poured it on her car and set it on fire. He turned around, and she was doubled over with tears running down her cheeks.

Enraged now, the truck driver screamed, "You're crazy! What's so funny?"

Through fits of laughter, the yuppette replied, "Every time you weren't looking, I stepped outside the circle!"

Following the directions

A young yuppette was sick and tired of all those yuppette stories and how all yuppettes were perceived to be shallow and dumb. She made up her mind that she would show her new husband that she was really smart.

One day while he was at work, she purchased a can of paint and decided to paint the living room.

Her husband arrived home at 5:30 and smelled the distinctive odor of paint. He walked into the living room and found his wife lying on the floor in a pool of sweat. He observed that she was wearing a ski jacket as well as a fur coat.

He went over to ask if she was OK. She acknowledged that she was. He then asked what she was doing.

She replied that she had set out to prove to him that not all yuppettes were dumb, and to do so, she had elected to paint the living room.

He then asked why she was wearing both a ski jacket and a fur coat. Her response was that she read the directions on the paint can, and they said, "For best results, put on two coats."

Two girls were being observed in a parking lot. They were working with a coat hanger and a locked Mercedes. Soon the first girl said, "Hurry up! It's starting to rain, and the top is down!"

An inexpensive pair of shoes

A young yuppette was on vacation in the back-country of Louisiana. She wanted a pair of genuine alligator shoes in the worst way, but she was very reluctant to pay the high prices the local vendors were asking. After becoming very frustrated with the "no haggle" attitude of one of the shopkeepers, the yuppette shouted, "Maybe I'll just go out and catch my own alligator so I can get a pair of shoes at a reasonable price!"

The shopkeeper responded, "By all means, be my guest. Maybe you'll luck out and catch yourself a big one!" Determined, the yuppette headed for the swamps, set on catching herself an alligator.

Later in the day the shopkeeper was driving home when he spotted the young woman standing deep in the water, shotgun in hand. Just then she saw a huge, nine-foot alligator swimming quickly toward her. She took aim and killed the creature and, with a great deal of effort, hauled it up on the swamp bank. Lying nearby were several more of the dead creatures.

The shopkeeper watched in amazement. Just then the yuppette flipped the alligator on its back and, frustrated, shouted out, "This one isn't wearing any shoes either!"

Worth the Price?

He: I got this great new hearing aid the other day.

She: Are you wearing it now?

He: Yes. Cost me four thousand dollars, but it's top of the line.

She: What kind is it?

He: Twelve-thirty.

―――――――――

Jimmy and Johnny, panting and pulling on their tandem bicycle, finally reached the top of a long, steep hill.

"Whew!" gasped Jimmy. "What a climb!"

"Sure was!" agreed Johnny. "If I hadn't kept the brake on, we'd have gone down backward."

Too much salt

A young military pilot spent six years in a Soviet salt mine after being shot down. One evening after his release, he was parked on Lover's Lane with his girlfriend. His girlfriend asked him what he thought about while he was in prison for six years, hoping it was she.

Without a pause, the young pilot startled her with his reply, "Pepper!"

Boasting

In San Jose, Costa Rica, there is a huge hospital covering two blocks. One day a cab driver picked up three passengers at the San Jose airport. The first one, from New York, bragged about how Yankee Stadium was built in less than two years.

The second, from Rome, spoke up and boasted that the Colosseum was built by slave labor in only ten months.

The third, a Texan, was not to be outdone. "Why, they built the Astrodome in six months."

About this time, they passed the huge hospital. "What is that building?" one asked.

"I don't know," answered the cab driver. "It wasn't there this morning."

During a history lesson, the teacher asked a student, "Stevie, do you believe that George Washington could have pitched a dollar across the Potomac River as the saying goes?"

The student looked up and quickly answered, "I guess so. Our history book says he pitched his camp across the Delaware River when the British were pursuing him."

A businessman called with a question about the documents he needed in order to fly to China. After a lengthy discussion about passports, I reminded him that he needed a visa.

"Oh, no, I don't. I've been to China many times and never had to have one of those," he responded.

I double-checked, and, sure enough, his stay required a visa. When I told him this he replied, "Look, I've been to China four times, and every time they have accepted my American Express card."

A fellow was found with a rope around his wrist, strung from a light fixture. His buddy cut him loose and said, "What do you think you are doing?"

"I'm committing suicide."

"You'd have to put the rope around your neck if you really wanted to commit suicide!"

"I already tried that, and it was choking me."

SHORT STORIES

A woman motorist was driving along a country road when she noticed a couple of repairmen climbing telephone poles. "Fools!" she exclaimed. "They must think I have never driven a car before!"

More funny stories

A college dean was berating a veteran economics professor for having used the same tests for the past thirty-five years. "Don't you realize, professor, that the students have been sharing these tests for decades and that all of your students know exactly what's on the test before they sit for it?"

"Doesn't matter," replied the professor. "I just keep changing the answers."

Short and funny

"That is Black Mountain?"

"Yes, sir, highest mountain around Lake George."

"Any story or legend connected with that mountain?"

"Lots of them. Two lovers once went up that mountain and never came down again."

"Indeed! Why, what became of them?"

"Went down the other side."

QUICKIES

A man asked, "Do these stairs take you to the third floor?"
The other person said, "No, you have to walk!"

A customer said to the salesman, "I want to try on that suit in the window."

The salesman said, "Oh, sir, we couldn't allow that. You have to use the dressing room like everyone else."

Recently, a woman went through three lights in a row. They were on the truck in front of her!

Quick observations

In 1920 the United States Post Office ruled that children could not be sent by parcel post. Makes you wonder what was going on before that ruling!

A friend of mine hates M&Ms because they are so hard to peel.

Thinking about life

Confucius say: To make egg roll, push it.

Why?

Why is the third hand on a watch called a *second hand*?

An accountant was having a hard time sleeping, so he went to see his doctor. "Doctor, I just can't get to sleep at night."

"Have you tried counting sheep?"

"That's the problem—I make a mistake and then spend three hours trying to find it!"

"With a car like that, my advice is to keep it moving," instructed the mechanic to the concerned owner.

"Why?" asked the owner.

"If you ever stop, the cops will think it's an accident."

two

LOVE AND MARRIAGE

FINDING THE RIGHT ONE

Men and dogs

What makes men chase women they have no intention of marrying?

The same urges that make dogs chase cars they have no intention of driving.

City slicker

My wife and I went to a "dude ranch" in Texas. The cowboy preparing the horses asked if she wanted a Western or English saddle, and she asked what the difference was.

When he told her one had a horn and one didn't, she replied, "The one without the horn is fine. I don't expect we'll run into too much traffic."

MAN, *with hands over the eyes of the woman*: If you can't guess who it is in three guesses, I'm going to kiss you.

WOMAN: Jack Frost, Santa Claus, and Christopher Columbus.

A feminist walked into a bar that had a sign marked, "For Men Only."

"I'm sorry, ma'am," said the bartender. "We only serve men in this place."

"Great!" she said, "I'll take two of them."

Stressing the importance of a large vocabulary, the English teacher told the class, "Use a word ten times, and it will be yours for life."

In the back of the room a pert young lady closed her eyes and was heard chanting under her breath: "Charles, Charles, Charles, Charles, Charles, Charles, Charles, Charles, Charles, Charles."

A young man was attempting to worm his way into the affections of a beautiful young lady. "I don't have as much as Bill Gates," he said. "I don't have expensive houses or cars like Bill Gates. I can't afford to buy you fancy diamonds and pearls like Bill Gates. But I love you."

The young lady said, "That's nice. Now tell me more about this Bill Gates."

HEADING DOWN THE AISLE

A man and a woman are standing at a cocktail party when the woman remarked, "You know, you look like my third husband."

"How many times have you been married?" asked the man.

"Twice!" replied the lady.

All in the family

Alicia was very impressed with her boyfriend's loving parents.

"They're so thoughtful," Alicia said one night to Michael. "Why, I've noticed that your dad even brings your mom a cup of hot coffee in bed every morning."

After a time, Alicia and Michael were engaged and then married.

On the way from the wedding to the reception, Alicia again remarked on Michael's loving parents and even mentioned the coffee in bed.

"Tell me," she said, "does it run in the family?"

"It sure does," replied Michael. "I take after my mother."

Polygamy

A little boy was attending his first wedding. After the service, his older cousin asked him, "Do you know how many women a man can marry?"

"Sixteen," the boy responded.

His cousin was amazed that he offered an answer so quickly.

"How do you figure that?"

"Easy," the little boy said. "All you have to do is add it up, like the preacher said: 'Four better, four worse, four richer, four poorer.'"

Weddings

Little Mary was at her first wedding and gaped at the entire ceremony. When it was over, she asked her mother, "Why did the lady change her mind?"

Her mother asked, "What do you mean?"

"Well, she went down the aisle with one man and came back with another one."

Quieting those nosy aunts

Old aunts used to come up to me at weddings, poking at me in the ribs and cackling, telling me, "You're next!"

They stopped doing that after I started doing the same thing to them— at funerals!

Marriage

Two women were discussing marriage, and one said, "My husband and I have been married twenty-five years, and every night my husband has complained about the food. We've had not one night without complaining about the food."

The other woman said, "That's awful. Doesn't it bother you?"

The first one said, "Not in the slightest."

Said the other woman, "You must be a saint."

To which the first woman replied, "No. Why should I object? Many people don't like the food they cook."

And the good news

A young woman brought her fiancé home to meet her parents. After dinner, her mother told her husband to find out about the young man. So the young woman's father took the young man into his study to discuss things "man to man."

"So, what are your plans, young man?" asked her father.

"I am a Bible scholar," the young man replied.

"A Bible scholar. *Hmm,*" the father said, "admirable, but what will you do to provide a nice house and life for my daughter?"

"I will study," the young man replied. "God will provide for us."

"And how will you buy her a beautiful engagement ring such as she deserves?" asked the father.

"I will concentrate on my studies," the young man answered. "God will provide for us."

"And children?" asked the father. "How will you support children?"

"Don't worry, sir. God will provide," replied the fiancé.

The conversation proceeded like this for quite an amount of time. Every time the father asked a question, the young man always replied with, "God will provide."

Later, after the young man had left, the mother asked her husband, "How did it go?"

The father answered, "He has no job and no plans, but the good news is he thinks I'm God."

Happy father of the bride

All eyes were on the radiant bride as her father escorted her down the aisle. They reached the altar and the waiting groom. Then the beautiful bride kissed her father and placed something in his hand.

That surprised the father so much that he dropped the object. He had not expected her to give him anything at the front of the church.

Ripples of laughter waved through the sanctuary as the guests watched as he bent down and picked up his credit card.

STARTING LIFE TOGETHER

Modern times

A recent bride called her mother one evening in tears. "Oh, Mom, I tried to make Grandmother's meat loaf for dinner tonight, and it turned out just awful. I followed the recipe exactly, and I know I have the recipe right because it's the one you gave me. But it just didn't come out right, and I'm so upset. I wanted this to be so special. What could I have done wrong?"

Her mother replied soothingly, "Well, dear, let's go through the recipe. You read it out loud and tell me exactly what you did at each step, and together we'll figure it out."

"OK," the bride sniffled. "Well, it starts out, 'Take fifty cents worth of ground beef.'"

NEW BRIDE: I fixed your favorite dessert for you tonight—coconut pudding. Wait until you see it.

NEW GROOM: Wow! That's great! But what's that big lump in the middle?

NEW BRIDE: That's the coconut.

Two can live as cheaply as one—for half as long.

Debugging

A couple honeymooned at the Watergate Hotel in Washington DC. The bride was concerned that the room was bugged, but the groom said, "Don't worry. I'll check." So he looked behind the drapes, behind the pictures, and under the rug. There he found a disc with four screws; he unscrewed them and threw them and the disc out the window. The next morning, the hotel manager asked, "How was your stay? How was your room? How was the service?"

"Why all these questions?" asked the groom.

"Well," explained the manager, "the people in the room under you complained of the chandelier falling on them."

A newly married couple returned from their honeymoon. As they got off the plane at the crowded airport, the bride said, "Darling, let's make the people think that we have been married a long time."

"OK, dear," said the husband. "You carry the bags."

Who's in control?

A husband was advised by a psychiatrist to assert himself. "You don't have to let your wife henpeck you. Go home and show her you are the boss," advised the psychiatrist.

Of course, the husband took the doctor's advice. He hopped in his car and rushed home. There he slammed the door, shook his fist in his wife's face, and growled, "Woman, from now on, you're taking orders from me. I want my supper right now, and when you get it on the table, go upstairs and lay out my best clothes. I'm going out with the boys, and you are going to stay at home where you belong. And here's another thing. Do you know who's going to comb my hair, adjust my pants, and then tie my bow tie?"

"I certainly do," said the wife calmly without even looking up. "The undertaker."

Male/female

Being silent is good. Others think you are listening.

A dangerous slip

"Well," said Eric, "I ran afoul of one of those questions women ask. Now I'm in deep trouble at home."

"What kind of question?" asked Tom.

"My wife asked me if I would still love her if she was old, fat, and ugly."

"That's easy," said Tom. "You just say, 'Of course I will.'"

"Yeah, that's easy for you to say. What I said was, 'Of course I do'!"

"Your Honor, my wife is just being ridiculous. Most women would love to have a husband who still believes in chivalry, and I was only opening the door for her out of chivalry."

"Mr. Smith," replied the judge, "I am granting the divorce. I cannot believe chivalry was your motivation while driving sixty-five miles per hour."

Pain relief

A man entered a drug store and asked the pharmacist for a cure for the hiccups. The pharmacist immediately reached out and slapped him across the face.

"What'd you do that for?" asked the man angrily.

"Well, you don't have the hiccups anymore, do you?"

"No," replied the man, "but my wife out in the car still does!"

Never satisfied

A prisoner escaped from the local prison. His escape was the lead news item on the six o'clock news, and all stations kept interrupting their programming to report on the hunt.

Because of the high level of hunting, the prisoner was forced to work his way home slowly by taking side streets and dark alleys.

Finally he crept up to his house and rang the doorbell. His wife immediately opened the door and greeted him with, "Where have you been? You escaped six hours ago!"

Answer

One evening, a wife drew her husband's attention to the couple next door. She took him out on the porch so he could see what they were doing. Pointing across the yard, she said, "Do you see that couple? How devoted they are? He kisses her every time they meet. I notice that he often brings home flowers or dinner. Why don't you ever do that?"

"I would love to," replied the husband amiably and smoothly, "but I don't know her well enough."

A tramp knocked on the door of the inn known as St. George and the Dragon. The landlady answered the door.

The tramp said, "Could you give a poor man something to eat?"

"No," said the woman, slamming the door in his face.

He knocked again and said, "Could I have a few words with George?"

But you could have

A husband and wife were traveling and stopped at a very exclusive hotel to rest for a while. They slept for four hours, then decided to leave and travel on. When they checked out, the desk clerk handed them a bill for $350.

The man exploded and demanded to know why the charge was so high. He demanded to see the manager.

The manager appeared, listened to the man, and then explained that the hotel had an Olympic-sized pool and a huge conference room that was available for their use.

"But we didn't use them," protested the man.

"Well, they are here, and you could have," said the manager. He went on to explain that they could have taken in one of the shows for which the hotel was famous.

"But we didn't go to any shows," argued the man.

"Well, we have them, and you could have," repeated the manager.

No matter what facility the manager mentioned, the man replied, "But we didn't use it!" Eventually the man realized he was going to have to pay, so he wrote a check.

"But, sir," the manager said, "this check is only for $100."

"That's right. I charged you for kissing my wife."

"But I didn't!"

"Well," the man replied with a wry smile, "she was here, and you could have."

Hurt feelings

At the fair, Marge loved the Ferris wheel, but Fred didn't, so Marge went by herself. The wheel went round and round. Suddenly there was an accident, and the wife was thrown out. She landed in a heap at her husband's feet. He ran over and asked, "Are you hurt?"

"Of course, I'm hurt!"

"Tell me, is there anything broken?" he asked anxiously.

"No, nothing's broken."

"Then how are you hurt?"

With tears in her eyes she blurted, "I went around three whole times, and you didn't wave to me once!"

O what a tangled web

One evening, a man drove his secretary home after she had worked late at the office. Although this was an innocent gesture, he did not mention it to his wife because he knew her jealous nature.

Later that night the man and his wife were driving out to dinner. Suddenly he noticed a high-heeled shoe half hidden under the passenger seat. Not wanting to be conspicuous, he waited until his wife was looking out her window before he scooped up the shoe and tossed it out of the car.

With a sigh of relief, he pulled into the restaurant parking lot. That's when he noticed his wife squirming around in her seat.

"Honey," she asked, "have you seen my other shoe?"

SQUIRMS OF ENDEARMENT

I was invited to some old friends' home for dinner.

The husband preceded every request to his wife with an endearing term, such as "honey," "darling," "sweetheart," "pumpkin," etc.

I was impressed since the couple had been married almost seventy years.

While the wife was off in the kitchen, I said to my older friend, "I think it's wonderful that, after all these years you've been married, you still call your wife those pet names."

My friend hung his head. "To tell you the truth," he said, "I forgot her first name about ten years ago."

Dave

A man walked out into the street and managed to get a taxi that was just going by. He got into the taxi, and the cabby said, "Perfect timing; you're just like Dave."

"Who?"

"Dave Bronson. There's a guy who did everything right. Like my coming along when you needed a cab…it would have happened like that to Dave."

"There are always a few clouds over everybody," the man replied.

"Not Dave. He was a terrific athlete. He could have gone on the pro tour in tennis. He could golf with the pros. He sang like an opera baritone and danced like a Broadway star."

"He was something, huh?"

"He had a memory like a trap. He could remember everybody's birthday, he knew which fork to eat with, and he could fix anything. Not like me. I change a fuse and black out the whole neighborhood."

"No wonder you remember him so well."

"Well, I never actually met Dave."

"Then how do you know so much about him?"

"I married his widow."

Unappreciated

One afternoon a man came home from work to find total mayhem in his house. His three children were outside, still in their pajamas, playing in the mud, with empty food boxes and wrappers strewn all around the front yard. The door of his wife's car was open, as was the front door to the house.

Proceeding into the entry, he found an even bigger mess. A lamp had been knocked over, and the throw rug was wadded against one wall. In the front room, the TV was loudly blaring a cartoon channel, and the family room was strewn with toys and various items of clothing.

In the kitchen, dishes filled the sink, breakfast food was spilled on the counter, dog food was spilled on the floor, a broken glass lay under the table, and a small pile of sand was spread by the back door. He quickly headed up the stairs, stepping over toys and more piles of clothes, looking for his wife.

He was worried that she might be ill or that something serious had happened. He found her lounging in the bedroom, still curled up in the bed in her pajamas, reading a novel.

"What happened here today?" he asked. "Are you OK?"

"Yes, I'm fine. You know, every day when you come home from work, you ask me what in the world I did all day. Well, today I didn't do it."

You know you're having a bad day when...

You call your spouse and tell her that you'd like to eat out tonight, and when you get home, you find a sandwich on the front porch.

FAMILY RELATIONS

A man was taking his wife, who was pregnant with twins, to the hospital when his car went out of control and crashed.

Upon regaining consciousness, he saw his brother, a relentless practical joker, sitting at his bedside.

"Don't worry," his brother assured him, "your wife and son and daughter are fine. I just left them. But the hospital was in such a hurry with the birth certificates that I had to name them for you. I named the girl Denise."

Relieved, the man responded, "Thank you. That's a pretty name. What did you name the boy?"

"Denephew."

———

"I watched my wife's routine at breakfast for years," the expert explained. "She made lots of trips between the refrigerator, stove, table, and cabinets, often carrying a single item at a time. One day I told her, 'Hon, why don't you try carrying several things at once?'"

"Did it save time?" the guy in the audience asked.

"Actually, yes," replied the expert. "It used to take her twenty minutes to make breakfast. Now I do it in seven."

———

Give a man a fish, and he will eat for a day. Teach a man to fish, and he will go out and buy expensive fishing equipment, stupid-looking clothes, a sports utility vehicle, travel a thousand miles to the "hottest" fishing hole, and stand waist deep in cold water just so he can outsmart a fish. (Average cost per fish: $395.68.)

Hearing

A man and his wife sat in their car after a quarrel. The man was so angry that he clammed up and refused to talk.

His wife, however, sat in the back seat and continued to berate him for his faults. In her excitement, she pounded on the car door, and it flew open.

Several blocks later, one of their neighbors flagged the man down.

"Your wife fell out of the car back there," he said.

The man looked over at the back seat, turned to this neighbor, and said, "Thank goodness! I thought I had lost my hearing!"

A guide, showing an old lady through the zoo, took her to a cage occupied by a kangaroo.

"Here, madam," he said rather pompously, "we have a native of Australia."

She replied, "And to think my sister married one of them."

Short ones

After she woke up, a woman told her husband, "I just dreamed you gave me a pearl necklace for Valentine's Day. What do you think it means?"

"You'll know tonight," he said.

That evening the husband came home with a small package and gave it to his wife. Delighted, she opened it—to find a book entitled *The Meaning of Dreams*.

WIFE TO SLEEPY HUSBAND: Charlie, wake up. It's garbage day!

HUSBAND: Oh, honey, just tell him we don't want any.

Push?

A loud pounding on the door awakened a man and his wife at 3:00 a.m. The man got up and went to the door to find a drunken stranger standing in the pouring rain. The drunken stranger asked for a push.

"Not a chance," answered the man. "It's three o'clock in the morning!" And he slammed the door and returned to bed.

After explaining the situation to his wife, she gently reminded him, "Don't you remember when we broke down on our vacation, and those two guys helped us? I think you should go help this guy."

Begrudgingly, the husband dressed and went outside to help the stranger. "Hello, are you still here?" he called.

"Yes," came the answer.

"Do you still need a push?"

"Yes, thanks."

"Where are you?"

"Over here—on the swing."

Experienced motherhood

I have five siblings: three sisters and two brothers. One night I was chatting with my mom about how she had changed as a mother from the first child to the last. She told me she had mellowed a lot over the years.

"When your oldest sister coughed or sneezed, I immediately called the ambulance," she explained. "When your youngest brother swallowed a dime, I just told him it was coming out of his allowance."

THE SECRET OF A LONG MARRIAGE

A couple was celebrating their golden wedding anniversary. Their domestic tranquility had long been the talk of the town. A local newspaper reporter was inquiring as to the secret of their long and happy marriage.

"Well, it dates back to our honeymoon," explained the husband. "We visited the Grand Canyon and took a trip down to the bottom of the canyon by pack mule. We hadn't gone too far when my wife's mule stumbled. My wife quietly said, 'That's once.' We proceeded a little farther when the mule stumbled again. Once more, my wife quietly said, 'That's twice.' We hadn't gone half a mile when the mule stumbled a third time. My wife promptly removed a revolver from her purse and shot the mule dead. I started to protest her treatment of the mule when she looked at me and quietly said, 'That's once.'"

three

CHUCKLE WITH CHILDREN

RAISING LITTLE ONES

If it was going to be easy to raise kids, it never would have started with something called *labor*.

Children finish proverbs
- Strike while…the bug is close.
- It's always darkest before…Daylight Savings Time.
- Never underestimate the power of…termites.
- You can lead a horse to water…but why?
- Don't bite the hand that…looks dirty.
- You can't teach an old dog…new math.
- The pen is mightier than…the pigs.
- Where there's smoke, there's…pollution.
- A penny saved is…not much.
- Don't put off till tomorrow what…you put on to go to bed.
- If at first you don't succeed…get new batteries.

A group of children were in the schoolyard bragging about their fathers. The first boy said, "My dad scribbled a few words on a piece of paper, called it a *poem*, and they gave him $50."

The second boy said, "That's nothing. My dad scribbled a few words on a piece of paper, called it a *song*, and they gave him $100."

The third boy said, "I got you both beat. My dad scribbled a few words on a piece of paper, called it a *sermon*, and it took eight people to collect all the money!"

Fourth graders complete

Laugh and the world laughs with you. Cry, and...someone yells, "Shut up!"

CHILDREN AND PRAYERS

I had been teaching my three-year-old daughter, Caitlin, the Lord's Prayer. For several evenings at bedtime, she would repeat after me the lines from the prayer.

Finally, she decided to go solo. I listened with pride as she carefully enunciated each word, right up to the end of the prayer:

"Lead us not into temptation," she prayed, "but deliver us some e-mail. Amen."

A little boy was overheard praying, "Lord, if you can't make me a better boy, don't worry about it. I'm having a real good time like I am."

KIDS AND RELIGION

A mother was preparing pancakes for her sons Kevin, age five, and Ryan, age three. The boys began to argue over who would get the first pancake. Their mother saw the opportunity for a moral lesson. "If Jesus were sitting here, He would say 'Let my brother have the first pancake; I can wait.'"

Kevin turned to his younger brother and said, "Ryan, you be Jesus!"

Short story

Little Johnny's new baby brother was screaming up a storm.

Johnny asked his mom, "Where'd we get him?"

"He came from heaven, Johnny."

"Wow! I can see why they threw him out!"

My grandson was visiting one day when he asked, "Grandma, do you know how you and God are alike?"

I mentally polished my halo while I asked, "No, how are we alike?"

"You're both old," he replied.

School

At the Henry Street Hebrew School, the rabbi finished the day's lesson. It was then time for the usual question period. "Rabbi," said little Walter, "there's something I need to know."

"What's that, my child?" asked the rabbi.

"Well, according to the Scriptures, the children of Israel crossed the Red Sea. Right?"

"Right."

"And the children of Israel beat up the Philistines. Right?"

"Right."

"And the children of Israel built the temple. Right?"

"Again, you are correct," reassured the rabbi.

"And the children of Israel fought the Egyptians, and the children of Israel fought the Romans, and the children of Israel were always doing something important. Right?"

"Yes. What's your question?"

"What I need to know," demanded Walter, "is where were all the grownups?"

Helpful?

A priest was walking down the street one day when he noticed a very small boy trying to press a doorbell on a house across the street. However, the boy was very small, and the doorbell was too high for him to reach.

After watching the boy's efforts for some time, the priest moved across the street and walked up behind the little fellow. Placing his hands kindly on the child's shoulder, he leaned over and gave the doorbell a solid ring. Crouching down to the child's level, the priest smiled benevolently and asked, "And now what, my little man?"

To which the boy replied, "Now we run!"

SCHOOL DAYS

Listening to teacher

A little kid started kindergarten. The teacher was trying to help the kids with their hygiene. "Remember, children, every day you must put on a clean pair of underwear."

The little kid took his teacher's words to heart. But by Saturday he found it difficult to get his jeans on.

Question

In class, the teacher was trying desperately to get the students to think. He asked, "If the Pilgrims were alive today, what would they be most famous for?"

One student quickly responded, "Their age."

Another silly question

The teacher posed a question: "George Washington not only chopped down his father's cherry tree, but he also admitted doing it. Now, do you know why his father didn't punish him?"

Quickly one of the students replied, "Because George still had the axe in his hand."

Kids' answers to test questions

- Name a major disease associated with cigarettes. *Premature death.*
- What is a terminal illness? *When you get sick at the airport.*

Help

Little Johnny's mother was called into the school one day by the principal. "We're worried about little Johnny," he said. "He goes around all day *cluck, cluck, clucking.*"

"That's right," said little Johnny's mother. "He thinks he's a chicken."

"Haven't you taken him to a psychiatrist?" asked the principal.

Little Johnny's mother replied, "Well, we would, but we really need the eggs."

Listening to kids

When my granddaughter Ann was nine years old, she was given an assignment by her teacher to write a story on, "Where My Family Came

From." The purpose for the assignment was to help the kids understand genealogy.

I was not aware of her assignment when she asked at the dining room table one night, "Grandma, where did I come from?"

I responded quite nervously because my son and daughter-in-law were out of town. I tried to stall until they returned home, "Well, honey, I'll tell you. The stork brought you."

"Where did Mom come from, then?"

"The stork brought her too."

"OK, where did you come from?" continued my granddaughter.

"The stork brought me too, dear."

"OK, thanks, Grandma," she replied as the conversation turned to another topic.

I did not think anything more about it until two days later when I was cleaning Ann's room and read the first sentence of her paper: "For three generations there have been no natural births in our family."

Ain't it the truth?

Mrs. Applebee, the sixth-grade teacher, posed the following problem to one of her arithmetic classes: "A wealthy man died and left ten million dollars. One-fifth was to go to his wife, one-fifth to his son, one-fifth to his butler, and the rest to charity. Now, what does each get?"

After a very long silence in the classroom, little Morris raised his hand.

The teacher asked him for his answer.

With complete sincerity in his voice, Morris answered, "A lawyer!"

The teacher asked little Sammy to tell the class what his father did for a living. "Oh, he's a magician. His best trick is sawing people in half."

"Wonderful!" said the teacher. "Are there other children in your family?"

"Yes, ma'am. I have two half brothers."

They are watching

The children were lined up in the cafeteria of a Catholic school for lunch. At the head of the long serving table was a large pile of apples. The nun made a sign, "Take only one. We are watching."

At the other end of the table was a large pile of chocolate chip cookies. One of the boys wrote a sign, "Take all you want. The nuns are watching the apples."

Brotherly love

The teacher asked a young boy this test question: "What would you do if you saw two trains doing fifty miles per hour approaching each other on the same track?"

The boy replied, "I would get a red lantern and wave it at them, warning them to stop."

"What if you had no lantern?"

The boy replied, "Then I'd wave a red handkerchief."

"What if you didn't have a red handkerchief?" asked the teacher.

"Then I would go get my younger brother."

"Why in the world would you get your younger brother?" asked the teacher.

"My younger brother," responded the student, "has never seen a big train wreck."

Miss Jones had been giving her second-grade students a lesson on science. She had explained about magnets and showed how they would pick up nails and other bits of iron. Now it was question time, and she asked, "My name begins with the letter *m*, and I pick up things. What am I?"

The little boy on the front row said, "You're a mother."

Kids vs. teachers

TEACHER: George, go to the map and find North America.

GEORGE: Here it is!

TEACHER: Correct. Now, class, who discovered America?

CLASS: George!

Kids and Adults Together

Sweet revenge

When little Johnny opened up one of the holiday presents from his grandmother, he discovered a water pistol. He squealed with delight and headed for the sink.

His mother was not so pleased. She turned to her mother and said, "I'm surprised at you. Don't you remember how we kids used to drive you crazy with water guns?"

Her mom smiled and then replied, "I remember quite distinctly."

A dinner party

During a dinner party, the hosts' two little children entered the dining room totally nude and walked slowly around the table. The parents were so embarrassed that they pretended nothing was happening and kept the conversation going. The guests cooperated and also continued as if nothing extraordinary was happening. After going all the way around the room, the children left. As they disappeared out of sight, there was a moment of silence at the table, during which one child was heard to say, "You see, it IS vanishing cream!"

Guaranteed to roll your eyes

A tourist on his way to Tuscaloosa came to a fork in the road and stopped. There was no sign indicating which route went where. Spotting a young boy by the road, he yelled out, "Hey! Kid! Does it matter which road I take to get to Tuscaloosa?"

"Not to me it doesn't," quickly replied the boy.

Mothers

Mom's definition: The speed of light is 186,000 miles per second, or the distance a baby can crawl when you turn your back.

More common sense

A man driving through the countryside passed a young boy walking along wearing only one shoe.

The man stopped and asked, "Did you lose a shoe?"

"Nope," replied the boy, "found one."

Remedy

Billie Jean went into the grocery store and asked for fifty gallons of milk. The clerk, amazed, asked her what she was going to do with that much milk. "I have a skin problem, and the doctor prescribed a milk bath."

The clerk asked, "Pasteurized?"

"No, just up to my chin."

Quickies

- Women should not have children after thirty-five. Really, thirty-five children are enough!
- I am a nobody. Nobody is perfect. Therefore, I am perfect!

Parental wisdom

When you have three young boys, it's hard to know who to blame if something goes wrong in the house. One father explained to a friend how he solved the problem: "I send all three to bed without letting them watch television. In the morning, I go after the one with the black eye!"

Kids

A four-year-old came in to the dentist for his first checkup. The dentist tried to strike up a conversation. "How old are you?" he asked.

Immediately four small fingers went up. Smiling, the dentist asked, "Can't you talk?"

The solemn little patient asked, "Why, can't you count?"

Kids' lyrics

- "God bless America through the night with a light from a bulb!"
- "O Susanna, O don't you cry for me; for I come from Alabama with a Band-Aid on my knee!"
- "Give us this day our deli bread! Glory be to the Father and to the Son and to the whole East Coast."
- "We shall come to Joyce's, bringing in the cheese."

Modern convenience

When I stopped the bus to pick up Chris for preschool, I noticed an older woman hugging him as he left his house. "Is that your grandmother?" I asked.

"Yes. She came to visit us for the holidays."

"How nice. Where does she live?"

"At the airport," Chris answered. "Whenever we want her, we just go out there and get her."

Photographers

Two weeks after my one-year-old's photo shoot, I returned to the studio to view the pictures on a color monitor. The photographer started describing the merits of each photo, but as he went through the set, he spoke so quickly that I couldn't get a word in.

Finally, after we'd seen all twenty poses, he asked me which ones I was most interested in.

"None," I replied. "That isn't my child."

One way

A woman answered her front door and found two little boys holding a list. "Lady, we're on a scavenger hunt, and we still need three grains of wheat, a pork-chop bone, and a piece of used carbon paper to earn a dollar."

"My goodness," the woman replied. "Who sent you on such a challenging hunt?"

"Our babysitter's boyfriend."

Childbirth knowledge

Q: What is the most reliable method to determine a baby's sex?

A: Childbirth.

Those who say they "sleep like a baby" don't have one.

The duel

A little boy came home from the playground with a bloody nose, black eye, and torn clothing. It was obvious he'd been in a bad fight and lost. While his father was patching him up, he asked his son what happened.

"Well, Dad," said the boy, "I challenged Larry to a duel. And, you know, I gave him his choice of weapons."

"Uh-huh," said the father, "that seems fair."

"I know, but I never thought he'd choose his big sister!"

A little boy kept looking at the rack of greeting cards. The clerk asked if she could help him—birthday? Illness? Wedding?

The boy shook his head no and answered wistfully, "Got anything in the line of blank report cards?"

A small boy in a department store was standing near the escalator, watching the moving handrail.

"Something wrong, son?" inquired a floorwalker.

"Nope," replied the boy. "Just waiting for my chewing gum to come back."

A boy walked up to the box office at a movie theater one Wednesday afternoon at one o'clock and handed the cashier the money for a ticket. "It's only one o'clock," she said to him as she handed over a ticket. "Why aren't you in school?"

"Oh, it's all right," he said. "I've got the measles."

Turnabout

It was a hectic day of running errands for a father, mother, and son. As if the stress weren't enough, four-year-old Chris insisted on asking questions about everything. He told his mother how to drive; he sang every song he knew. Finally, fed up with his incessant chatter, the dad made him an offer, "Christopher, if you'll be quiet just a few minutes, I'll give you a quarter."

It worked. But when the family stopped for lunch, the dad unknowingly began to harp on his son. "Christopher, sit up straight...don't spill your drink...don't talk with your mouth full."

Finally Christopher looked at his father and said, "Dad, if you'll be quiet just a few minutes, I'll give you a quarter."

Three boys were bragging about their fathers.

The oldest spoke first and said in a loud voice, "My dad's so fast he can shoot an arrow and get to the target before the arrow does!"

"That's nothing!" said the second boy in an even louder voice, "My dad's so fast he can shoot a deer at five hundred yards and get to that deer before it falls!"

"Big deal!" said the third in the loudest voice of the three. "My dad can beat either of those two. His work shift ends at 4:30, and he's so fast he gets home at 3:45!"

Roles

Whenever I'm disappointed with my spot in my life, I stop and think about little Jane Scott. Jane was trying out for a part in a school play. Her mother told me that she'd set her heart on being in it, though she feared she would not be chosen. On the day the parts were awarded, I went with her mother to get Jane after school.

Jane rushed up to her mother, eyes shining with pride and excitement. "Guess what, Mom," she shouted, and then said those words that will remain a lesson to me: "I've been chosen to clap and cheer."

After going into escrow for a larger house, the couple told their seven-year-old that they had to move because another baby was coming.

"Aw, that won't work," frowned the youngster. "He'll just follow us."

School term report card: "Your son's handwriting is so bad we cannot tell whether he can spell or not."

four

PARENTING PREDICAMENTS

BIRDS AND BEES?

An old country doctor went out in the country to deliver a baby where there was no electricity. When he arrived, no one was home except the laboring mother and her five-year-old son.

The doctor needed assistance, so he recruited the young boy to help. He instructed the child to hold a lantern high so he could see while he delivered the baby. The child took his job quite seriously.

The mother pushed, and, after a while, the doctor lifted the newborn baby by the feet and spanked him on the bottom to get him to take his first breath. The doctor then looked at the little boy.

"Hit him again," the child said. "He shouldn't have crawled up there in the first place!"

Expecting

Four expectant fathers were in a hospital waiting room while their wives were in labor. The nurse arrived and proudly announced to the first man, "Congratulations, sir. You're the father of twins!"

"What a coincidence! I work for the Twins baseball team."

Later the nurse returned and congratulated the second father on the birth of his triplets.

"Wow! That's incredible! I work for the 3M Company."

An hour later, the nurse returned to congratulate the third man on the birth of his quadruplets.

Stunned, he barely could reply, "I don't believe it! I work for the Four Seasons Hotel!"

After this, everyone turned to the fourth guy, who had just fainted. The nurse rushed to his side. As he slowly regained consciousness, they could hear him mutter over and over, "I should never have taken that job at 7-Eleven. I should never have taken that job at 7-Eleven. I should never have taken..."

KIDS SAY THE CUTEST THINGS

Daddy's trick

The little boy greeted his aunt with a hug and said, "I'm glad to see you! Now maybe Daddy will do the trick he has been promising to do."

The aunt was curious. "What trick is that?"

The little boy replied, "I heard Daddy tell Mommy that he would climb the walls if you came to visit us again."

Concerned neighbor

Worried that they hadn't heard anything for days from the widow in the apartment next door, the mother said to her son, "Tony, would you go next door and see how old Mrs. Rock is?"

A few minutes later, Tony returned.

"Well, is she all right?" asked the mother.

"She's fine, but she's rather annoyed with you," answered Tony.

"At me?" exclaimed the mother. "Whatever for?"

Tony replied, "Mrs. Rock said it's none of your business how old she is."

Female logic

A little girl had just finished her first week of school. "I'm just wasting my time, she said to her mother. "I can't read, I can't write, and they won't let me talk!"

TEENAGERS

A teen just got his driver's license and asked his father for the keys.

"Son," replied his father, "after you get your grades up, start reading your Bible every day, and get a haircut, I'll let you drive the car."

A little time went by, and the son repeated his request. "And Father, I'm getting better grades, and I'm reading the Bible every day!"

"Indeed you are," his father responded, "but you still haven't gotten a haircut."

"Aw, Dad. Samson had long hair, and so did Moses. In fact, Jesus had long hair too!"

"Yes, son, and they walked everywhere they went!"

Wrong number

Late one Saturday evening, the ringing of my phone awakened me. The party on the other end of the line paused for a moment before rushing breathlessly into a lengthy speech. "Mom, this is Susan, and I'm sorry I woke you up, but I had to call because I'm going to be a little late getting home. See, Dad's car has a flat, but it's not my fault. Honest! I don't know what happened. The tire just went flat."

I interrupted to explain that I didn't have any daughters. "Sorry, dear, but I have to tell you you've reached the wrong number. I don't have a daughter named Susan. In fact, I don't have any daughter at all." There was a long pause.

"Mom," came the young woman's quavering voice, "I didn't think you'd be this mad."

During one "generation gap" quarrel with his parents, a young man cried, "I want excitement, adventure, money, romance. I'll never find it here at home, so I'm leaving. Don't try to stop me!"

With that he headed toward the door, his parents close behind.

"Didn't you hear what I said? I don't want you to stop me!"

"Who's stopping you?" replied his parents. "We're going with you!"

Teenage concern

The teenage beauty was telling a friend that she was really worried about her mother. The friend inquired as to the reason for her worrying. The teenage beauty informed her friend that her mom was always fatigued from staying up all night long.

Her friend asked, "What's she doing staying up all night? At her age, that's not good at all!"

The beauty answered, "Waiting for me to come home."

Teenage priority

Two teenagers were arrested for public nuisance when they were found smoking in the fountain in the town square. The arresting officer told them they were entitled to a phone call since he was unable to reach any parent.

Some time later, a man entered the station and asked for the boys by name.

The desk officer said, "I suppose you're the kids' lawyer?"

"Nope," the chap replied, "I'm just here to deliver the pizza they ordered."

Obvious explanation

A teenage girl had been talking on the phone for about half an hour when she hung up. "Wow!" said her father. "That was short. You usually talk for two hours. What happened?"

"Wrong number," explained the girl.

Time warp

A college student wrote a letter home:

> Dear folks, I feel miserable cause I have to keep writing for money. I feel ashamed and unhappy. I have to ask for another hundred, but every cell in my body rebels. I beg on bended knee that you forgive me. Your son, Marvin
>
> PS: I felt so terrible I ran after the mailman who picked this up at the box at the corner. I wanted to take this letter and burn it. I prayed to God that I could get it back, but I was too late.

A few days later, he received a letter from his father:

> Dear Son, Good news! Your prayers were answered. Your letter never came!

OH, THOSE PARENTS

Wrong number

A woman meant to call a record store but dialed the wrong number and got a private home instead. "Do you have 'Eyes of Blue' and 'A Love Supreme'?" she asked who she thought was a clerk.

"Well, no," answered the puzzled homeowner. "But I have a wife and eleven children."

"Is that a record?" she inquired.

"I don't think so," replied the man, "but it's as close as I want to get."

No help

My friend's preparations for a visit from her children included a trip to the bank. Waiting in line at the teller's window, she lamented to the middle-aged man behind her, "My children are in their twenties, and I'm still giving them money. When does it end?"

"I'm not sure I'm the one to ask," the man said while glancing uncomfortably at a paper in his hand. "I'm here to deposit a check from my mother."

———————

MAN: "This is my wife's birthday. I'd like to buy her a beautiful fountain pen."

SALESPERSON: "A surprise, eh?"

MAN: "You bet; she's expecting a Cadillac."

Mothers' remarks

- Mona Lisa's mother: "After all that money your father and I spent on braces, that's the biggest smile you can give us?"
- Columbus's mother: "I don't care what you've discovered! You could have written!"
- Michelangelo's mother: "Can't you paint on walls like other children? Do you have any idea how hard it is to get that stuff off the ceiling?"
- Mary's mother: "I'm not upset that your lamb followed you to school, but I would like to know how he got a better grade than you."
- Einstein's mother: "But it's your senior picture. Can't you do something about your hair? Styling gel, mousse, something?"
- Washington's mother: "The next time I catch you throwing money across the Potomac, you can kiss your allowance good-bye!"
- Jonah's mother: "That's a nice story. Now tell me where you've really been."
- Edison's mother: "Of course I'm proud that you invented the electric light bulb. Now turn it off and go to bed!"

Parental observations

There would be fewer problems with children if they had to chop wood to keep the television going.

five

SHORT AND TO THE POINT

GREAT TRUTHS ABOUT LIFE THAT ADULTS HAVE LEARNED

- Families are like fudge—mostly sweet with a few nuts.
- Raising teenagers is like nailing Jell-O to a tree.
- Carsickness is the feeling you get when the monthly car payment is due.

Wise saying

It isn't difficult to make a mountain out of a molehill; just add a little dirt.

Punster thinking

Half of a large intestine: 1 semicolon.

INTERESTING SIGNS

- Outside a muffler shop: "No appointment necessary. We hear you coming."
- In a veterinarian's waiting room: "Be back in five minutes. Sit! Stay!"
- At the electric company: "We would be de-lighted if you send in payment for your bill. However, if you don't, you will be."
- In a restaurant window: "Don't stand there and be hungry. Come on in and get fed up."
- In the front yard of a funeral home: "Drive carefully. We'll wait."
- Pizza shop slogan: "Seven days without pizza makes one weak."
- On a plumber's truck: "We repair what your husband fixed."
- In a nonsmoking area: "If we see smoke, we will assume you are on fire and take appropriate action."

- At an optometrist's office: "If you don't see what you're looking for, you've come to the right place."
- In a podiatrist's office: "Time wounds all heels."
- On a fence: "Salesmen welcome! Dog food is expensive!"
- At a pizza shop: "Buy our pizza. We knead the dough."
- At a tire shop in Milwaukee: "Invite us to your next blowout."
- At a car dealership: "The best way to get back on your feet—miss a car payment."
- In a health-food shop: "Closed due to illness."

Sign that you're at a bad fast-food place

The sign out front reads, "No shirt, no shoes, no reason you can't get a job here."

Bumper Stickers

- A word to the wise is sufficient, but who can remember the word?
- You can't tell which way the train went by looking at the tracks.
- It was a brave man who ate the first oyster.
- Why is the man who invests all your money called a *broker*?
- Why do croutons come in airtight packages? It's just stale bread to begin with.
- Take my advice; I'm not using it.
- We have enough youth! How about a fountain of smart?
- Do you believe in love at first sight, or shall I drive by again?
- I don't eat snails; I prefer fast food.
- I'm a driver cleverly disguised as a responsible adult. Please honk if anything falls off.
  - Life not only begins at forty; it also begins to show.
  - Old skiers never die; they just go downhill.

Church Bulletin Funnies

"Bertha Belch, a missionary from Africa will be speaking tonight at Memorial Church. Come tonight and hear Bertha Belch all the way from Africa."

Church marquee

- Worry is interest paid on trouble before it is due.
- Under same management for thousands of years.

Church bulletin bloopers

- Ushers will eat latecomers.
- Miss Mason sang, "I Will Not Pass This Way Again," giving obvious pleasure to the congregation.
- The cost for attending the Fasting and Prayer Conference includes meals.

Did You Know?

- Like fingerprints, everyone's tongue print is different.
- A duck's quack doesn't echo, and no one knows why.
- Over 75 percent of people who read this will try to lick their elbow.

Life's little reminders

Life is like a mirror; we get the best results when we smile at it.

———

Birthdays are good for you—the more you have, the longer you live.

———

How can you tell when you run out of invisible ink?

Q: Why do mountain climbers rope them-
     selves together?
A: To prevent the sensible ones from going
     home.

I don't know how I got over the hill without getting to the top.

Thoughts
Some mistakes are too much fun to make only once.

I just received a new state quarter. It's two dimes and a nickel taped together.

Last night I dreamed I was a muffler—I woke up exhausted!

If Cain and Abel were Siamese twins, would they be Cable?

On my first day of school, my parents dropped me off at the wrong nursery. There I was…surrounded by trees and bushes.

The trouble with being a leader today is that you can't be sure whether people are following you or chasing you.

Why is it that rain drops but snow falls?

"We may be lost," the husband said to his wife, "but at least we're making good time."

Hard work may not kill you, but why take chances?

Inserts

If at first you don't succeed, then skydiving is not for you.

Never pick a quarrel, even when it's ripe.

Are you telling the truth when you lie in bed?

When I sing, people clap their hands—over their ears.

- Blessed are those who hunger and thirst, for they are sticking to their diets.
- Every time I think about exercise, I lie down until the thought goes away.
- This sign was posted in a Grand Rapids furniture store: "Try Our Easy Payment Plan—100% Down—Nothing Else to Pay."

Want a surefire way to get your kids to play with their old toys? Have a garage sale.

Considerations

- Why don't we get goose bumps on our faces?
- The only place you can find success before work is in the dictionary.

You know it's going to be a bad day when...
- You call suicide prevention, and they put you on hold.
- You turn on the news, and they are showing escape routes out of the city.
- Your twin sister forgets your birthday.
- Your income tax check bounces.
- You put both contacts in one eye.
- Your birthday cake collapses from the weight of the candles.

Weird things you'd never know
- Elephants are the only animals that can't jump.
- Women blink nearly twice as often as men.
- A dentist invented the electric chair.
- All polar bears are left-handed.
- A crocodile cannot stick its tongue out.
- *Typewriter* is the longest word that can be made using the letters only on one row of the keyboard.

Dilbert's Rule of Order
When you don't know what to do, walk fast and look worried.

Bits and pieces
- Middle age: When actions creak louder than words.
- Two silkworms were in a race. They ended up in a tie.

FUNNY QUOTES

"If Noah had been wise, he'd have swatted those two flies."—Helen Castle

------

There are two ways to reach the top of an oak tree—you can climb it, or you can sit on an acorn and wait.

The real art of a conversation is not only to say the right thing in the right place, but also to leave unsaid the wrong thing at the tempting moment.

The road to success is dotted with many tempting parking places.

ONLY IN AMERICA

- …can a pizza get to your house faster than an ambulance.
- …are there handicap parking places in front of a skating rink.
- …do people order double cheeseburgers, large fries, and a Diet Coke.
- …do banks leave both doors to the vault open and then chain the pens to the counters.
- …do we leave cars worth thousands of dollars in the driveway and put our useless junk in the garage.
- …do we use answering machines to screen calls and then have call waiting so we won't miss a call from someone we didn't want to talk to in the first place.

Thoughts

A sign under a mounted fish: "If I had kept my mouth shut, I wouldn't be here."

Frequent naps prevent old age, especially if taken while driving.

Spotted on the back window of a small car being pulled by a motor home: "I go where I'm towed."

Snowmen fall from heaven unassembled.

Simple rule

Don't throw bricks straight up.

RIDDLES

Q: What do you say to a hitchhiker with one leg?
A: Hop on in.

This and that

How come wrong numbers are never busy?

Q: Why are there so many Smiths in the phone book?
A: They all have phones.

Q: Why did the turtle cross the road?
A: To get to the Shell station.

Q: What is a small joke called?
A: A mini-Ha!-Ha!

Q: What did one hair say to the other?
A: It takes two to tangle.

Q: What did the sea say to the sand?
A: Not a thing; it just waves.

Q: What makes a tree so noisy?
A: Its bark.

The meek shall inherit the earth—after we're through with it, of course.

Ever notice that a human baby doesn't walk until it's tall enough to reach a parent's hand?

Did You Know...

It's impossible to sneeze with your eyes open.

Thoughts

The grass may seem greener on the other side, but both sides still need to be mowed.

Warning notice at a seminary swimming pool: "First-year-students are only allowed to walk on the shallow end."

GEOGRAPHY TEACHER: Who can describe the English Channel?
STUDENT: We don't get that channel on our TV.

All things being equal, big people use more soap.

By the time you can make ends meet, they move the ends.

Facts of life

- You're getting old when you get the same sensation from a rocking chair that you once got from a roller coaster.
- God put me on Earth to accomplish a certain number of things. Right now I am so far behind, I will live forever.
- Brain cells come and brain cells go, but fat cells live forever.
- Amazing! You just hang something in your closet for a while, and it shrinks two sizes.
- Inside some of us is a thin person struggling to get out, but he or she can usually be sedated with a few pieces of chocolate cake.

It's so hot in Texas that...

- The birds have to use potholders to pull the worms out of the ground.
- Farmers are feeding their chickens crushed ice to keep them from laying hard-boiled eggs.
- The cows are giving evaporated milk.

Printed on the back of a leather jacket worn by a motorcyclist: "If you can read this, my girlfriend fell off."

If you want the world to beat a path to your door, try taking a nap on Saturday afternoon.

Faith Statement: Speaking of ailments, don't!

The equator is an imaginary lion running around the world.

six

JOKE THEOLOGY 101

LIVING IN FAITH

My grandmother, who lived in Tucson, was well known for her faith and her lack of reticence in talking about it. She would go out on the front porch and yell, "Praise the Lord!"

Her next-door neighbor would shout back, "There ain't no God!" During those days, my grandmother was very poor, so the neighbor decided to prove his point by buying a large bag of groceries and placing it at her door.

The next morning, Grandmother went to the porch and, seeing the groceries, said, "Praise the Lord!"

The neighbor then stepped out from behind a tree and said, "I bought those groceries, and there ain't no God."

Grandmother replied, "Lord, You not only sent me food, but You made the devil pay for it."

Take me out to the ball game.

Two buddies, Bob and Earl, were two of the biggest baseball fans ever. For their entire adult lives, they discussed baseball history in the winter and pored over every box score during the season. They even agreed that whoever died first would try to come back and tell the other if there was baseball in heaven. One summer night, Bob passed away in his sleep after watching a Yankee victory. A few nights later, his buddy Earl awoke to the sound of Bob's voice. "Bob, is that you?" asked Earl.

"Of course it's me."

Earl exclaimed, "So tell me, is there baseball in heaven?"

"Well, I have good news and bad news," said Bob. "The good news is there's baseball in heaven."

"And the bad news?" asked Earl.

"Tomorrow night, Earl, you're pitching."

Ad-libbing

A college drama group presented a play in which one character would stand on a trapdoor and announce, "I descend into hell!"

A stagehand below would then pull a rope, the door would open, and the character would plunge through. The play was well received. One night the usual actor fell ill, and the substitute was quite overweight. When the new actor announced, "I descend into hell," he became stuck in the trap door. No amount of tugging on the rope could make him descend. One student in the balcony yelled, "Hallelujah! Hell is full!"

A modern-day scientist was conversing with God and told Him blatantly, "You know, God, we can transplant just about every organ; we can replace arms and legs and so forth. It seems to me we just don't need You anymore, God."

God, in His quiet way, replied, "Well, you think not, huh? Let's just have a contest and make a man."

"OK." And the scientist enthusiastically reached down and grabbed up a handful of dirt.

"Oh, no," God stopped him in midair. "Get your own dirt!"

Practical lad

A little child in church for the first time watched as the ushers passed the offering plates. When they neared the pew where he sat, the youngster piped up so that everyone could hear, "Don't pay for me, Daddy. I'm under five."

As an atheist walked through the forest, he smiled at the beauty that was all around him and said, "What natural wonders the powers of evolution have created." Just then he heard a rustling near the river. He went to investigate and a seven-foot-tall grizzly bear was tearing down the path toward him.

The man took off like a shot, and when he got up the courage to look back, he saw the bear was catching up fast. He tried with all his strength to pick up the pace, but he tripped and crashed to the ground. As he tried to get up, the bear jumped on his chest and picked up one paw to whack him. The atheist screamed, "Oh, my God!"

Time stopped! The bear froze. The forest was silent. Even the river stopped moving. As a bright light shone upon the man, a voice boomed from the heavens, "You deny My existence for all of these years, teach others I don't exist, and even credit creation to a cosmic accident. Do you expect Me to help you out of this predicament? Am I to count you as a believer?"

The atheist looked directly into the light. "It would be hypocritical of me to suddenly ask You to treat me as a Christian now, but could You perhaps make the bear a Christian?"

"Very well," the voice said. The light went out, the river ran again, and the sounds of the forest resumed. And then the bear dropped its right paw, brought both paws together, bowed its head, and spoke: "Lord, for this food that I am about to receive, I am truly thankful."

One of life's lessons

While preaching about forgiving one's enemies, the preacher asked for a show of hands of those who were willing to forgive their enemies. About half of the congregation raised their hands. The minister continued his lecture and again asked for a show of hands. This time, 80 percent of his congregation raised their hands. Not giving up, the minister continued for fifteen more minutes. When he again asked for a show of hands, all members—except one—raised their hands.

"Mr. Jones," asked the minister, "are you not willing to forgive your enemies?"

"I don't have any."

"Mr. Jones, that is very unusual. I know you are eighty-six years old. Would you please come down to the front and explain to all of us how you have lived so long without making a single enemy in the world?"

Mr. Jones teetered to the front and briefly explained, "It's easy. I've outlived every one of them."

Prayers not answered

Years ago when my two girls were small, they were taught how to say their blessing before eating their meal. One night as I was busy scurrying around the kitchen, I told them both to say their blessings without me. I took a moment to watch them as they both squeezed their eyes tightly shut over folded hands. As my four-year-old finished, her three-year-old sister kept on praying.

Another minute or two passed before she lifted her head, looked at her plate, and in an indignant voice said, "Hey! My peas are still here!"

Address error

Consider the case of the Illinois man who left the snow-filled streets of Chicago for a vacation in Florida. His wife was on a business trip and was planning to meet him there the next day. When he reached his hotel, he decided to send his wife a quick e-mail.

Unfortunately, when typing her address, he missed one letter, and his note was directed instead to an elderly preacher's wife whose husband had passed away only the day before. When the grieving widow checked her e-mail, she took one look at the monitor, screamed, and fell to the floor in a dead faint.

At the sound, her family rushed into the room and saw this note on the screen: "Dearest wife, Just got checked in. Everything prepared for your arrival tomorrow. P.S. Sure is hot down here."

This and that

My therapist insists that the way to achieve true inner peace is to finish what I start. So far today, I have finished two bags of M&Ms and a chocolate cake—I feel better already.

Why is that when you talk to God you're praying, but when He talks to you, you're crazy?

Just checking

A five-year-old said grace at a family dinner one night. "Dear God, thank You for these pancakes."

When he concluded, his parents asked him why he thanked God for pancakes when they were having chicken.

He smiled and said, "I thought I'd see if He was paying attention tonight."

The two men were adrift in an open boat, and it looked bad for them. Finally one of them, frightened, began to pray. "O Lord," he prayed, "I've broken most of Thy commandments. I've been a hard drinker, but if my life is spared now I'll promise never again…"

"Wait a minute, Jack," said his friend. "Don't go too far. I think I see a sail."

Spendthrifts

A father and his son were looking at a nativity scene in a London gallery. It was Titian's world-famous painting of the scene at Bethlehem. The boy said, "Dad, why is the baby lying in such a crude cradle in a pile of straw?"

"Well, son," explained the father, "they were poor, and they couldn't afford anything better."

Said the boy, "Then how could they afford to have their picture painted by such an expensive artist?"

The VIP

The pope had just finished a tour of the East Coast and was taking a limousine to the airport. Having never driven a limo, he asked the chauffeur if he could drive for a while. Well, the chauffeur didn't have much of a choice, so the chauffeur climbed in the back of the limo and the pope took the wheel.

The pope proceeded to hop on I-95 and started accelerating to see what the limo could do. He got to about ninety miles per hour and *WHAM!* There were the blue lights of the friendly state patrol in his mirror. The pope pulled over, and the trooper came to his window. Well, the trooper, seeing who it was, said, "Just a minute, please. I need to call in."

The trooper radioed in and asked for the chief. He told the chief, "I've got a VERY important person pulled over, and I need to know what you want me to do."

The chief replied, "Who is it? Not the senator again?"

The trooper said, "No, even more important."

"It isn't the president, is it?"

"No, more important."

"Well, WHO is it?" screamed the chief.

"I don't know," said the trooper, "but whoever he is, he's got the pope as his chauffeur."

BIBLE HUMOR

Q: Is baseball recorded in the Bible?

A: Yes. In the BIG-inning, Rebekah took the pitcher to the well, David struck out Goliath, and the prodigal son made a home run.

Q: What time of day was Adam created?

A: Right before Eve.

Q: The ark's top-story windows opened to the sky for light and air. How did Noah get light to the dark recesses of the ark?

A: He used floodlights.

Q: Why couldn't Cain please God with his sacrifice?

A: Because he wasn't Abel.

Q: Who was the wealthiest male financier in the Bible?

A: Noah. He was floating his stock while everybody else was in liquidation.

Q: Where is the first tennis match mentioned in the Bible?

A: When Joseph served in Pharaoh's court.

All I really needed to know, I learned from Noah's ark.

- Plan ahead. It wasn't raining when Noah built the ark.
- Stay fit. When you're six hundred years old, someone might ask you to do something really big.
- Don't listen to critics—do what has to be done.
- Build on high ground.
- For safety's sake, travel in pairs.
- If you can't fight or flee—float!
- Don't forget that we're all in the same boat.
- Don't miss the boat.

Bible quiz

Q: What kind of man was Boaz before he married?

A: Ruthless.

Q: What do they call pastors in Germany?

A: German shepherds.

Q: What kind of motor vehicles are in the Bible?

A: Jehovah drove Adam and Eve out of the garden in
    a Fury. David's Triumph was heard throughout the
    land. And Honda, because the apostles were all in one
    Accord.

Q: What excuse did Adam give to his children as to why
    he no longer lived in Eden?

A: "Your mother ate us out of house and home."

Q: What servant of God was the most flagrant
    lawbreaker in the Bible?

A: Moses—he broke all Ten Commandments at once.

Q: What area of Palestine was especially wealthy?

A: The area around Jordan. The banks were always over-
    flowing.

Q: Who is the greatest babysitter mentioned in the Bible?

A: David. He rocked Goliath to a very deep sleep.

Q: What Bible character had no parents?

A: Joshua, son of Nun.

There was a very gracious lady who was mailing an old family Bible to
her brother in another part of the country. "Is there anything breakable in
here?" asked the postal clerk.

"Only the Ten Commandments," answered the lady.

A pastor moved into a new town and went out one Saturday to visit his
neighbors. All went well until he came to one house. It was obvious that
someone was home, but no one came to the door even after he knocked
and knocked and knocked.

Finally he took out his business card and wrote on the back, "Revelation 3:20," and stuck it in the door. (Revelation 3:20 reads: "Behold, I stand at the door, and knock: if any man hear my voice, and open the door, I will come in to him, and will sup with him, and he with me.")

The next day one of the ushers came up to him after the service and gave the pastor that same card. Below his message of Revelation 3:20 was Genesis 3:10. (Here was the reply from Genesis 3:10: "I heard thy voice...and I was afraid, because I was naked.")

A ten-year-old, under the tutelage of her grandmother, was becoming quite knowledgeable about the Bible. Then one day she floored her grandmother by asking, "Which virgin was the mother of Jesus—the Virgin Mary or the King James Virgin?"

KID'S VIEWS OF THE OLD TESTAMENT

- Adam and Eve were created from an apple tree.
- Noah's wife was called Joan of Ark.
- Noah built the ark, and the animals came on in pears.
- Moses went up on Mount Cyanide to get the Ten Amendments.
- The Fifth Commandment is humoring thy father and mother.

Biblical question

A father was reading Bible stories to his young son. He read, "The man named Lot was warned to take his wife and flee out of the city, but his wife looked back and was turned to salt."

His son asked, "But what happened to the flea?"

THE PASTOR AND HIS FLOCK

Nothing personal

"I hope you didn't take it personally, Reverend," an embarrassed woman said after a church service, "when my husband walked out during your sermon."

"I did find it rather disconcerting," the preacher replied.

"It's not a reflection on you, sir," insisted the churchgoer. "Ralph has been walking in his sleep ever since he was a child."

Two men crashed in their private plane on a South Pacific island. Both survived. One of the men brushed himself off and then proceeded to run all over the island to see if they had any chance of survival. When he returned, he rushed up to the other man and screamed, "This island is uninhabited, there is no food, there is no water. We are going to die!"

The other man leaned back against the fuselage of the wrecked plane, folded his arms, and responded, "No, we're not. I make over $100,000 a week."

The first man grabbed his friend and shook him. "Listen, we are on an uninhabited island. There is no food, no water. We are going to die!"

The other man, unruffled, again responded, "No, I make over $100,000 a week."

Mystified, the first man, taken aback with such an answer, again repeated, "For the last time, I'm telling you, we are doomed. There is no one else on this island. There is no food. There is no water. We are, I repeat, we are going to die."

Still unfazed, the first man looked the other in the eyes and said, "Don't make me say this again. I make over $100,000 per week. I tithe 10 percent. My pastor will find us!"

A minister told his congregation, "Next week I plan to preach about the sin of lying. To help you understand my sermon, I want you all to read Mark 17."

The following Sunday as he prepared to deliver his sermon, the minister asked for a show of hands. He wanted to know how many had read Mark 17. Every hand went up.

The minister smiled and said, "Mark has only 16 chapters. I will now proceed with my sermon on the sin of lying."

The poor country pastor was livid when he confronted his wife with the receipt for a $250 dress she had bought. "How could you do this!" he exclaimed.

"I don't know," she wailed. "I was standing in the store looking at the dress. Then I found myself trying it on. It was like the devil was whispering to me, 'Gee, you look great in that dress. You should buy it.'"

"Well," the pastor persisted, "you know how to deal with him! Just tell him, 'Get behind me, Satan!'"

"I did," replied his wife. "But then he said, 'It looks great from back here too.'"

One Sunday after church a mom asked her very young daughter what the lesson was about. The daughter answered, "Don't be scared; you'll get your quilt." Needless to say, the mom was perplexed.

Later in the day, the pastor stopped by for tea, and the mom asked him what that morning's Sunday school lesson had been about. He said, "Be not afraid; thy comforter is coming."

Good news/bad news

A minister stood in front of his congregation and announced, "I have good news and bad news. The good news is we have enough money to pay for our new building program. The bad news is that it's still in your pockets."

Watching the signs

A local priest and pastor stood by the side of the road holding up a sign that read, "The end is near! Turn yourself around now before it's too late!" They planned to hold up the sign to each passing car.

"Leave us alone, you religious nuts!" yelled the first driver as he sped by.

From around the curve, they heard a big splash.

"Do you think," said one clergyman to the other, "we should just put up a sign that says 'Bridge Out' instead?"

Right answer (kind of)

The pastor was talking to a group of young children about being good and going to heaven. At the end of his talk, he asked, "Where do you want to go?"

"Heaven!" they all piped up.

"And what do you have to do to get there?" asked the pastor.

"Be dead!" shouted one little boy.

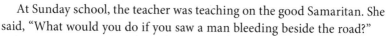

At Sunday school, the teacher was teaching on the good Samaritan. She said, "What would you do if you saw a man bleeding beside the road?"

A student jumped up and said, "I'd faint!"

What an answer

A pastor, known for his lengthy sermons, noticed a man get up and leave during the middle of his message. The man returned just before the conclusion of the service.

Afterward the pastor asked the man where he had gone. "I went to get a haircut," was the reply.

"But," said the pastor, "why didn't you do that before the service?"

"Because," the gentleman replied, "I didn't need one then."

At Sunday school they were teaching how God created everything, including human beings. Little Johnny, a child in the kindergarten class, seemed especially intent when they told him how Eve was created out of one of Adam's ribs.

Later in the week his mother noticed him lying on his bed as though he were ill. She said, "Johnny, what is the matter?"

Little Johnny responded, "I have a pain in my side. I think I'm going to have a wife!"

Praise and worship was really rocking in a Spirit-filled church of about two thousand when a hooded terrorist appeared at the sanctuary entrance with an automatic weapon. Shouting loudly he said, "All right, all you who are ready to die for your Christ can stay right where you are!" Immediately, hundreds upon hundreds rose to flee out of every exit.

When about twenty-five were left in the sanctuary, the disguised associate pastor removed his hood and announced, "OK, Pastor, we got rid of all the lukewarm Christians. Now you can begin your sermon!"

The artist

A Sunday school teacher began her lesson with the question, "Boys and girls, what do we know about God?"

A hand shot up in the air, "I know! I know! He's an artist!" said one little boy.

"Really? How do you know that?" asked the puzzled teacher.

"Oh, you know—'Our Father, who does art in heaven.'"

Groaner

The custodian of a church quit, and the pastor of the church asked the organist if she would be able also to clean the church sanctuary.

The organist thought before replying, "Do you mean that I now have to mind my keys and pews?"

Give us this day

The CEO of Smith Foods arranged a meeting with the head of a powerful church. "Reverend," he said, "Smith Foods is prepared to donate $100 million to your church if you change the Lord's Prayer from, 'Give us this day our daily bread,' to 'Give us this day our daily chicken.'"

The minister responded, "That is impossible. The prayer is permanent; it must not be changed."

"OK. We at Smith Foods respect your faith, but we do have one more offer. We will give the church $500 million."

Later, the minister met with his elders with the good news: "We have come into $500 million." And the bad news: "We're losing the Wonder Bread account."

Prayer

Three preachers sat discussing the best positions for prayer while a telephone repairman worked nearby. "Kneeling is definitely best," claimed one.

"No," another contended. "I get the best results standing with my hands outstretched to heaven."

"You're both wrong," the third insisted. "The most effective prayer position is lying prostrate, face down on the floor."

The repairman could contain himself no longer. "Hey, fellas," he interrupted. "The best prayin' I ever did was hangin' upside down from a telephone pole."

More short ones

After the birth of their child, an Episcopal priest, wearing his clerical collar, visited his wife in the hospital. He greeted her with a hug and a kiss, and gave her another hug and kiss when he left. Later, the wife's roommate commented, "Your pastor is sure friendlier than mine."

Bible knowledge

A Sunday school teacher asked her students to draw a picture of their favorite Old Testament story. As she moved around the class, she saw there were many wonderful drawings being done. Then she came across the drawing of one little boy. He was busy drawing a man driving an old car. In the backseat were two passengers—both scantily dressed.

"It's a lovely picture," prompted the teacher, "but which story does it tell?"

The little boy seemed surprised at the question. "Well," he exclaimed, "doesn't it say in the Bible that God drove Adam and Eve out of the Garden of Eden?"

Church humor

"If absence makes the heart grow fonder," said a minister, "a lot of folks must love our church."

Mother's orders

One Sunday morning, a mother knocked on her son's door and told him it was time to get up and go to church.

"I'm not going to church this morning," the son replied.

"You gotta get up and go to church," said the mother.

"No, I'm not," said the son.

"Yes, you are," said the mother.

"No, I'm not. They don't like me, and I don't like them. Give me two good reasons why I have to go."

"Number one, you're fifty-five years old, and number two, you're the pastor!"

The sure cure

Three pastors in the South were having lunch in a diner.

One said, "You know, since summer started, I've been having trouble with bats in my loft and attic at church. I've tried everything—noise, spray, cats—nothing seems to scare them away."

Another said, "Me, too. I've got hundreds living in the belfry and in the narthex attic. I've even had the place fumigated, and they won't go away."

The third said, "I baptized all mine and made them members of the church. Haven't seen one back since!"

My home church welcomes all denominations, but mainly they prefer tens and twenties.

A big mistake

An IRS agent went into a minister's study. "Pastor," he said, "do you know a Mr. Karten?"

"Yes, I do."

"Is he a member of your congregation?"

"Yes, he is."

"Did he make the $100,000 donation he's claiming on his return?"

"I assure you that he will!"

Answering prayers

The Wednesday night church service coincided with the last day of hunting season. During the service, our pastor asked who had bagged a deer. No one raised a hand.

Puzzled, the pastor said, "I don't get it. Last week many of you said you wouldn't be at church Sunday because of hunting season. I had the whole congregation pray for your deer."

One hunter said, "Well, preacher, it worked. They're all safe."

Knowing the subject

A Sunday school teacher was teaching her young students about Noah and the ark. She asked them what they thought Noah must have done to pass the time in the ark for forty days. After waiting a few moments, the teacher suggested, "Maybe he did a lot of fishing. How about that?"

One little boy gave her a funny look and said, "I don't think so. It's kinda hard to fish with just two worms!"

A minister asked a group of children in Sunday school class, "Why do you love God?"

He received a variety of answers, but the one he liked best was, "I don't know, sir. I guess it just runs in our family."

Shorties

In his Sunday morning sermon, a preacher recently announced that there are 726 different kinds of sin. Since that Sunday morning, he has been besieged with requests for the list, mostly from people who are afraid that they are missing something.

A Sunday school teacher challenged her children to take some time on Sunday afternoon to write a letter to God. They were to bring back their letter the following Sunday.

One little boy wrote, "Dear God, We had a good time at church today. Wish You could have been there."

"I've been racking my brains, but I can't place you," one man said to another at a gathering. "And you look very much like somebody I have seen a lot—somebody I don't like, but I can't tell you why. Isn't that strange?"

"Nothing strange about it," the other man said. "You have seen me a lot, and I know why you resent me. For two years I passed the collection plate in your church."

The church service was over. The pastor stood at the door shaking hands with the people as they left. A woman shook his hand and said,

"You know what? I don't think I'll come back anymore. Every time I come, either you sing 'He Arose' or 'Silent Night, Holy Night.'"

HUMOR IN HEAVEN

A man and his wife died and went to heaven at the same time. When they walked in, St. Peter said, "And this is your mansion," showing them a beautiful fifty-room mansion. The man said, "Who is going to pay the light bill?"

St. Peter said, "It's all paid!"

Then he showed them a beautiful lake and their own personal boat. The man said, "Well, who is going to pay the gas bill for the boat?"

St. Peter said, "It's all paid."

Then he took them to a beautiful golf course, and the man said, "But who is going to pay the greens fee?"

St. Peter said, "It's all paid for."

By that time, the man took his hat off, threw it on the floor, stomped on it, and said to his wife, "We would have been here a lot sooner if you hadn't fed us all those vitamins!"

For years, Archie and Jack argued about whether Jesus was white or black. Archie was certain Jesus was white, but Jack was just as certain He was black. As fate would have it, they both died on the same day and raced to the pearly gates to see who was right.

"St. Peter," they shouted, "is Jesus white or black?"

About that time Jesus walked up and said, "Buenos días."

A conversation with God

A young man was having a conversation with God. "God, how much is a million dollars worth to You?" he asked.

God replied, "To Me, it would be worth but a penny."

Then the young man asked, "How much is a million years to you?"

God answered, "Why, it would only be a second in eternity."

The young man paused to gather up his courage. "Then God," he continued, "could I have a million dollars, please?"

To which God replied, "Wait just a second."

Getting into heaven

Forrest Gump went before St. Peter at the Golden Gate. St. Peter welcomed Forrest, but said, "You need to answer three questions correctly before I can allow you to come into heaven. The first question is, 'How many *T*s are there in a week?'"

Forrest thought for just a second and replied, "There's two—today and tomorrow."

"That's not what I expected," replied St. Peter. "But I can't say you're wrong. The second question is, 'How many seconds in a year?'"

Forrest thought for a little bit and answered, "12—January 2nd, February 2nd, etc."

St. Peter scratched his head, shrugged, and again admitted that he'd have to accept that unusual answer. "Now," said St. Peter, "for the third question: 'What is God's first name?'"

This time Forrest did not hesitate at all. "Andy," he replied.

"Forrest, this time I just can't accept that answer. Can you explain it?"

"Sure," instantly replied Forrest. "It's in the church song—'*Andy* walks with me, *Andy* talks with me.'"

Too little, too late

A man arrived at the Pearly Gates, waiting to be admitted. St. Peter opened the gate and said, "I've been checking your file. I can't see that you did anything really good in your life, but you never did anything bad either. I'll tell you what—if you can tell me one really good deed that you did, I'll admit you."

So the man answered, "Once I was driving down the road and saw a gang of thugs attacking a poor man along the side of the road. So I pulled over, got out of my car, grabbed a tire iron, and walked straight up to the gang's leader—a huge, ugly guy with a chain running from his nose to his ear. Undaunted, I ripped the chain out of his ear and smashed him over the head with the tire iron. Then I turned around and, wielding my tire iron, yelled to the rest of them, 'You all leave this poor man alone! Go home before I teach you a lesson you'll never forget!'"

Impressed, St. Peter asked, "Really? I can't seem to find this in your file. When did all this happen?"

"Oh, about two minutes ago."

Fond memories

Tragically, three friends died in a car crash and found themselves at the gates of heaven. Before entering, they were each asked the same question by St. Peter: "When you are in your casket and friends and family are mourning for you, what would you like to hear them say about you?"

The first guy said, "I would like to hear them say that I was a great doctor of my time and a great family man."

The second guy said, "I would like to hear that I was a wonderful husband and schoolteacher who made a huge difference in our children of tomorrow."

The last guy replied, "I would like to hear them say, 'Look, he's moving!'"

Things under consideration

Why does everyone want to go to heaven, but I don't know anybody who wants to die?

seven

NUTRITIONAL HUMOR

I'm Taking Care of Myself

I walked around the block three times this morning…then I picked up the block and threw it in the toy chest.

Americans are getting stronger. Twenty years ago, it took two people to carry ten dollars' worth of groceries. Today, a five-year-old can do it.

One fellow walked into a doctor's office, and the receptionist asked him what he had. "Shingles," he said. So she took down his name, address, and medical insurance information and told him to have a seat.

Fifteen minutes later, a nurse's aide came out and asked him what he had. "Shingles," he said. So she took down his height, weight, and complete medical history and told him to wait in the examining room.

A half hour later a nurse came in and asked him what he had. "Shingles," he said. So she gave him a blood test, a blood pressure test, and an electrocardiogram. Then she told him to take off all his clothes and wait for the doctor.

An hour later the doctor came in and asked him what he had. "Shingles," he said.

The doctor said, "Where?"

He said, "Outside in the truck. Where do you want them?"

The best vitamin for a Christian is B_1.

Yes, it works

A man realized he needed to purchase a hearing aid, but he felt unwilling to spend much money. "How much do they run?" he asked the clerk.

"That depends," said the salesman. "They run anywhere from $2 to $2,000."

"Let's see the $2 model."

The clerk put the device around the man's neck. "You just stick this button in your ear and run this string down to your pocket," he instructed.

"How does it work?" the customer asked.

"For $2 it doesn't work," the salesman replied. "But people talk louder after seeing the string."

Stereotypes

On a stifling hot day, a man fainted in the middle of a busy intersection. Traffic quickly piled up in all directions, and a woman rushed to help him. When she knelt down to loosen his collar, a man emerged from the crowd, pushed her aside, and said, "It's all right, honey; I've had a course in first aid."

The woman stood up and watched as he took the ill man's pulse and prepared to administer artificial respiration. At this point, the woman tapped him on the shoulder and said, "Excuse me, when you get to the part about calling a doctor, I'm already here."

To tell the truth

Some members of a health club were having their first meeting. The director said, "Now, I'd like each of you to give the facts of your daily routine."

Several people spoke, admitting their excesses. Then one obviously overweight member said, "I eat moderately, I drink moderately, and I exercise frequently."

"*Hmm*," said the manager. "And are you sure you have nothing else to add?"

"Well, yes," admitted the member. "I lie extensively."

If people were not meant to have late-night snacks, why did God put a light in the refrigerator?

Why do drugstores make the sick walk to the back of the store for prescriptions, while healthy people buy cigarettes up front?

Short and cute

A practical medical school in Switzerland gave each graduating student a batch of ten-year-old copies of *TIME* magazine—so patients wouldn't think they were new in the business.

Employment applications always ask who is to be notified in case of emergency. I always write, "A very good doctor."

PAM: Did you hear about the new chocolate bar called *Jaws*?

SAM: No, I haven't. What does it cost?

PAM: An arm and a leg.

A well-done compliment

The customer called the waiter over and said, while pointing to his steak, "Didn't I tell you, 'Well done'?"

The waiter replied, "Thank you, sir; I seldom get a compliment."

Do it yourself

The other day it was my turn to prepare dinner, so I asked my wife to go over to the local market to buy some organic vegetables. She came back rather upset. It took her a while to settle down before she could explain why she was so upset.

Finally she explained, "I don't think I like that produce guy. I went and looked around for your organic vegetables. When I couldn't find them, I asked him for help. He didn't know what I was talking about, so I said, 'These vegetables are for my husband. Have they been sprayed with any poisonous chemicals?'

"And he said, 'No, ma'am. You'll have to do that yourself.'"

A man walking along the road saw an Indian with his ear to the ground. He went over and listened.

The Indian said, "Large wheels, Ford pickup truck, green color. Man driving with police dog next to him. Colorado license plate and traveling about seventy-five miles per hour."

The man was amazed and said, "You can tell all that just by listening with your ear to the ground?"

"Ear to the ground nothing," the Indian said. "That truck just ran over me!"

Medical history

A ninety-five-year-old woman had a baby, thanks to medical technology. She agreed to be interviewed by many local media companies and agreed that they could all come one afternoon to meet her and the little one.

That afternoon, local and national newspaper and TV companies invaded her house. The small cottage was overrun with relatives and reporters.

After interviewing the new mom, the interviewers asked to see the baby.

"Not yet," answered the new mother.

After more questions, the reporters again asked to see the new baby.

"Not yet," sweetly replied the new mother.

"Well," complained the reporters, "when can we see the baby?"

"When she cries. I forgot where I put her."

Good advice

A man walked into a restaurant in a strange town. The waiter came over to get his order. Feeling lonely, the man replied, "Meat loaf and a kind word." When the waiter returned with the meat loaf, the man said, "Where's the kind word?"

The waiter bent down and whispered, "Don't eat the meat loaf."

New on the job

Why did the new nurse buy red magic markers before reporting for work on her first day? She wanted to be prepared in case she needed to draw blood.

This and that

A panhandler walked up to a well-dressed woman who was shopping on Main Street and said, "Lady, I haven't eaten anything for four long days."

She looked at him and said, "I wish I had your willpower."

In pain

While working as a navy nurse in a military hospital, Anna was required to introduce herself by her rank and full name. She usually introduced herself as Ensign Anna Payne, but one day she rushed into a patient's room and blurted, "Hi, I'm Ensign Payne."

The patient slowly responded, "I'm in some pain too."

Herbs for youth

At a health-food store a man asked for an all-around herbal combination. The owner recommended one he said he'd sold for over sixty years.

Dubious, the fellow took the bottle to the cashier, a really stunning young lady. As he was paying, he asked, "Has your boss really been selling this stuff for sixty years? He looks to be a lot younger than I am."

"Can't really say, sir," replied the young woman. "I've only been working with him for forty years."

Healthy birth

Bill had lived all his life in a city of smog-spewing factories. All his life he had been frail and sickly. After his parents died, he decided to move to a healthier climate out West. So he packed up his few belongings and settled in Phoenix, Arizona.

On his first day there, he took advantage of the beautiful skies and clean air to go for a walk in a local park. There he sat down on a bench to enjoy the day. Soon a very healthy and good-looking young man sat down on the bench beside him.

"Say," said Bill, "is Phoenix really as healthful as it seems?"

"It sure is," replied the good-looking young man. "Why, when I came here I couldn't say one word. I had hardly any hair on my head. I didn't even have the strength to walk across a room. I was so weak I had to be lifted out of my bed."

"Goodness!" said Bill. "How long have you been here?"

With a smile on his face, the young man answered, "Since I was born."

A really nice place?

Between her sophomore and junior years at college, my daughter Laurie waited tables at a rather seedy steakhouse. One evening she waited on a well-dressed young couple. In a rather condescending tone, the man asked her, "Tell me, have you ever thought of going to college?"

"Actually, I do go to college," Laurie politely replied.

"Well, I went to Harvard," he said surveying the restaurant, "and I'd never work in a place like this."

"I go to Vassar," Laurie retorted, "and I make it a point to never eat in a dump like this."

Feeling good (really)

Farmer Joe decided his injuries from an accident were serious enough to take the trucking company whose truck caused the accident to court. In court, the trucking company's lawyer questioned Farmer Joe. "At the scene of the accident, didn't you say 'I'm fine'? And now you're claiming injury?"

"Well, let me explain," began Farmer Joe.

"No need to explain. Just answer the question."

At that point, the judge interrupted and allowed Farmer Joe to explain.

"Thank you, Your Honor," said Farmer Joe. "I had just loaded Bessie into the trailer and was driving down the highway when this huge semi-truck and trailer ran the stop sign and smacked my truck right in the side. I was thrown into one ditch and Bessie into the other. I was hurting real bad and didn't want to move. However, I could hear Bessie moaning, and I knew she was in trouble. Soon a highway patrolman came up, walked over to Bessie, saw her extreme condition, and shot her between the eyes to put her out of her misery. Then he came across the road to me. He had his gun in his hand, looked at me, and said, 'Your cow was in such bad shape that I had to shoot her. How are you feeling?' Naturally I looked up, saw the gun, and answered, 'I'm fine, really, I'm fine.'"

Solution

Tom had been a compulsive worrier for years until he found a way to overcome this problem. His friends noticed the dramatic change. "You don't seem to be worried about anything anymore."

"I hired a professional worrier for $1,000 a week," Tom replied. "I haven't had a single qualm since."

"A thousand a week! I know you don't have enough money to pay that kind of bill!"

"That's his problem," calmly replied Tom.

Making the grade

First, I got angina pectoris and then arteriosclerosis. Just as I was recovering from these, I got tuberculosis, double pneumonia, and ptilosis. Then they gave me hypodermics. Appendicitis was followed by tonsillectomy. These gave way to aphasia and hypertrophic cirrhosis. I completely lost my memory for a while. I know I had diabetes and acute ingestion, besides gastritis, rheumatism, lumbago, and neuritis.

I don't know how I managed to get through it all. It was the hardest spelling test I'd ever had.

Misunderstanding

"Waiter, come here at once," the agitated diner called. "Can you explain why there is a footprint in the middle of my food?"

"Yes, sir. You ordered an omelet and told me to step on it."

Hunger

The restaurant where I took my kids for a meal was crowded with fans watching a sporting event on television. A harried waitress took our order, but more than half an hour passed with no sign of her return.

I was trying to keep my kids from becoming restless, when suddenly shouts of victory came from the bar. "Hey, Dad!" commented my youngest. "It sounds like someone just got their food!"

Dying of thirst

A traveler was stumbling through the desert, desperate for water, when he saw something far off in the distance.

Hoping to find water, he walked toward the image, only to find a little old peddler sitting at a card table with a bunch of ties laid out for sale. The parched wanderer asked, "Please, I'm dying of thirst. Can I have some water?"

The man replied, "I don't have any water, but why don't you buy a tie? Here's one that goes nicely with your clothes."

The desperate man shouted, "I don't want a tie, you nut! I need water!"

"OK, don't buy a tie. But to show you what a nice guy I am, I'll tell you that over that hill there about five miles is a nice restaurant. Walk that way. They'll give you all the water you want."

The man thanked the peddler and walked away toward the hill and eventually disappeared out of sight.

Three hours later, he returned to the table where the man sat with the ties.

The man at the card table asked, "I told you—about five miles over that hill. Couldn't you find it?"

"I found it all right. They wouldn't serve me without a tie."

Free advertising

John told all his friends about the great steak he'd eaten downtown the day before. A group of them decided to head down to see if it really was as large and delicious as John was making it out to be. The group was seated in the back of the restaurant. After looking over the menu, they ordered and waited, hungrily, for their large, delicious pieces of gigantic steaks. To their collective disappointment, the waiter brought out some of the smallest steaks they'd ever seen.

"Now see here," a very embarrassed John said to the waiter. "Yesterday when I came here you served me a big, juicy steak. Today, though, when I have invited my friends, you serve small miniature steaks! What is the meaning of this?"

"Well, sir," replied the waiter, "yesterday you were sitting by the window."

The gourmet

A sign in the restaurant window read: "We can fix any dish you ask for. If we don't have it, you will be paid $200." Thinking that was a pretty good deal, the man went in and sat down at a table.

The waitress came over to take his order. He said, "I'll have roast elephant on rye bread; hold the mayo."

The waitress snapped her gum, stuck her pencil back in her hair, and walked into the kitchen. All of a sudden, the man heard screaming and yelling, pots and pans being thrown and dishes breaking. The kitchen door slammed open as the owner came charging out.

He put two one-hundred-dollar bills on the table and said, "I can't believe it. I've been in business here for ten years, and this is the first time I've run out of rye bread."

A little boy's prayer: "Dear God, please take care of my daddy and mommy and my sister and my brother and my doggy and me. Oh, please take care of Yourself, God. If anything happens to You, we're gonna be in a big mess."

"I will take a meal out occasionally, but I never go to the same restaurant twice," a man remarked.

To which his friend quickly replied, "I don't leave a tip either."

I'm on a Diet

Good reply

A successful diet is the triumph of mind over platter.

Stress diet for women

Breakfast: 1 grapefruit, 1 slice whole-wheat toast, 1 cup skim milk

Lunch: small portion of lean, steamed chicken; cup of spinach; cup of herbal tea; 1 Hershey kiss

Afternoon snack: the rest of the kisses in the bag; tub of Häagen-Dazs ice cream with chocolate-chip topping

Dinner: 2 loaves of garlic bread; 1 family-size supreme pizza; 3 Snickers bars

Late-night snack: whole frozen Sara Lee cheesecake (eaten directly from freezer)

Diet thoughts

- The most fattening thing you can put in a banana split is a spoon.
- The toughest part of a diet isn't watching what you eat. It's watching what other people eat.
- Dieting: going to some length to change your width.

- Most people gain weight by having intimate dinners for two...alone.

Thoughts

The older you get, the tougher it is to lose weight, because by then your body and your fat have become good friends.

The biggest seller is cookbooks, and the second is diet books about how not to eat what you've just learned to cook.

The hand of God

An overweight business associate of mine decided it was time to shed some excess pounds. He took his new diet seriously, even changing his driving route to avoid his favorite bakery. One morning, however, he arrived at work carrying a gigantic coffeecake. We all scolded him, but his smile remained cherubic.

"This is a very special coffeecake," he explained. "I accidentally drove by the bakery this morning, and there in the window was a host of goodies. I felt this was no accident, so I prayed, 'Lord, if you want me to have one of those delicious coffeecakes, let me have a parking place directly in front of the bakery.' And sure enough," he continued, "the eighth time around the block, there it was!"

Shorties

"May I take your order?" the waiter asked.

"Yes, how do you prepare your chicken?"

"Nothing special, sir," he replied. "We just tell them straight out that they're going to die."

Musings

If carrots are so good for the eyes, how come I see so many dead rabbits on the highway?

Rules of chocolate

How do you get two pounds of chocolate home from the store in a hot car? Eat in the parking lot.

Diet tip: Eat a chocolate bar before each meal. It'll take the edge off your appetite.

A nice box of chocolates can provide your total intake of calories in one place. Isn't that handy?

I've started a new exercise program. Immediately after waking in the morning, I always say sternly to myself, "Ready? Now up, down, up, down." And after two strenuous minutes I tell myself, "OK, now let's try the other eyelid!"

Kid kwickies

"What will you do when you are as big as your father?"

"Diet," replied the young boy.

Larry's girlfriend hit him with a tough line: "Larry, you're the salt of the earth, but, unfortunately, I need to cut the sodium out of my diet."

Friend to friend: "My dad still has the first two loaves of bread I baked for him. He uses them for bookends."

Those Medical Professionals

Losing a patient

While waiting for my first appointment in the reception room of a new dentist, I noticed his certificate, which bore his full name. Suddenly, I remembered that a tall, handsome boy with the same name had been in my high school class almost fifty years ago.

Upon seeing him, however, I quickly discarded any such thought. This balding, gray-haired man with the deeply lined face and stooped posture was too old to have been my classmate, I decided.

After he had examined my teeth, I asked him if he had attended the local high school.

"Yes," he replied.

"When did you graduate?" I asked.

He answered, "In 1955."

"Why, you were in my class!" I exclaimed happily.

He looked at me closely and then asked, "What subject did you teach?"

Three short puns

As the X-ray tech walked down the aisle to say the marriage vows with her former patient, a co-worker nurse whispered to a doctor seated next to her, "Wonder what she saw in him?"

Easy solution

Ken sought medical aid because he had bulging eyes and a persistent ringing in his ears. A doctor looked him over and suggested removing his tonsils. The tonsillectomy resulted in no improvement.

Ken then consulted a dentist, who suggested that removing his teeth might eliminate the problem. All of Joe's teeth were extracted, but still his eyes bulged out and the annoying ringing in his ears continued.

A third doctor told him bluntly, "You have six months to live."

Feeling doomed and gloomy, Ken decided to treat himself right while he still had time, so he bought a flashy car, hired a chauffeur and a gardener, and was measured by a tailor for some new suits. To go along with the new suits, he decided that even his shirts would be made to order.

"OK," said the shirt maker, "let's get your measurements. *Hmm*, thirty-four sleeve, sixteen collar..."

"No, I wear a fifteen collar," Ken corrected him.

"Sixteen collar," the shirt maker repeated, measuring again.

"But I've always worn a fifteen collar," said Ken.

"Listen," said the shirt maker, "I'm telling you right now—if you keep on wearing a tight fifteen collar, your eyes will bulge out, and you'll have ringing in your ears."

Medical instructions

A man went to his doctor and told him that he wasn't feeling well.

The doctor examined him, left the room, and came back with three bottles of pills. He told his patient, "Take the green pill with a big glass of water when you get up. Take the blue pill with a big glass of water after lunch. Just before going to bed, take the red pill with another big glass of water."

Startled at being put on so much medicine, the man stammered, "My goodness, Doc, exactly what's my problem?"

The doctor replied, "You're not drinking enough water."

A visit to the doctor

Whenever I accompanied my aunt on her visits to the doctor, she would complain to me about the long delay she always endured. It seemed inevitable that—no matter when she scheduled her appointment—she'd have to wait.

One day when my aunt's name was finally called, she was asked to step on the scale.

"I need to get your weight today," explained the nurse.

Without a moment's hesitation, my aunt replied, "One hour and forty-five minutes."

A day late

A doctor knocked on his patient's hospital door one evening. The doctor told him he had good news and bad news.

"What's the good news, Doc?" asked the patient.

"I'm sorry to have to tell you, but you have only twenty-four hours to live," answered the doctor.

"Whoa...Doc! If that's the good news, what's the bad news?" asked the anxious patient.

"I meant to tell you yesterday," replied the doctor.

Professionals

While attending a convention, three psychiatrists took a walk. "People are always coming to us with their guilt and fears," one psychiatrist said, "but we have no one to go to with our problems. Since we're all professionals, why don't we hear each other out right now? After all, if we can't trust each other, who can we trust?"

They agreed to this.

The first psychiatrist confessed, "I'm a compulsive shopper and deeply in debt, so I usually overbill my patients as much as I can."

The second admitted, "I have a drug problem that's out of control, and I frequently pressure my patients into buying illegal drugs for me."

The third psychiatrist said, "I know it's wrong, but no matter how hard I try, I just can't keep a secret."

Some common sense

An old man limped into the doctor's office and said, "My knee hurts so bad I can hardly walk!"

The doctor slowly eyed him from head to toe, paused, and then said, "Sir, how old are you?"

"I'm ninety-eight," the man announced proudly.

The doctor just sighed and looked at him again. Finally he said, "Sir, I'm sorry. I mean, just look at you. You are almost one hundred years old, and you're complaining that your knee hurts? Well, what did you expect?"

The old man replied, "Well, young man, my other knee is ninety-eight years old too, and it doesn't hurt!"

Etiquette

A pediatric nurse entered one of the examination rooms to give an immunization shot to a little girl.

When the little girl saw the nurse enter, she began screaming, "No! No! No!"

"Lizzie," her mother scolded, "that's not polite behavior."

At that, the girl yelled louder, "No, thank you! No, thank you! No, thank you!"

Doctor, doctor

"Doctor," whined the patient. "I keep seeing spots before my eyes."

"Why have you come to me? Have you seen an ophthalmologist?"

"No," replied the patient, "just these spots."

If all the people who fell asleep in church were laid end to end, they'd be much more comfortable.

Help, please

Sophie went to see a psychiatrist about her husband (he wouldn't go with her).

"Doctor, my husband has this problem—almost every night now he dreams he's a refrigerator!"

"My dear," replied the psychiatrist, "that is not really a problem. Many people dream that they are somebody or something unusual."

Sophie leaned forward as she softly whispered, "But you see, doctor, it is a problem for me! Jake sleeps with his mouth open, and the little light keeps me awake all night."

Modern medicine

A man who had just undergone a very complicated operation kept complaining about a bump on his head and a terrible headache. Since his operation had been an intestinal one, there was no earthly reason why he should be complaining of a headache. Finally the nurse spoke to his doctor about it.

"Don't worry about a thing, nurse," the doctor assured her. "He really does have a bump on his head. Halfway through the operation we ran out of anesthetic."

Clever lad

Because of an ear infection, my young son had to go to the pediatrician. We were new in town, and this was our first trip to our new doctor. I was impressed by the way the doctor directed his comments and questions to my son.

"Is there anything you are allergic to?" he asked Casey.

Casey nodded, leaned over to the doctor, and whispered in his ear.

Smiling, the pediatrician wrote out a prescription and handed it to me. Without looking at it, I tucked it into my purse.

Later, the pharmacist filled the order, remarking on the unusual food and drug interaction my son must have. When he saw my puzzled expression, he showed me the label on the bottle.

As per the doctor's instructions, it read, "Do not take with broccoli."

Doctor, doctor

A yuppette went into the doctor's office. "Doctor, you've got to help me. No matter where I touch my body, I experience horrible pain," she complained.

"Impossible," says the doctor. "Show me."

She took her finger and pushed on her elbow, screaming in agony. She then pushed on her knee and screamed, then on her ankle, screaming again.

And so it went. No matter where she touched, her agony was apparent.

The doctor said, "Your problem is not really as difficult as you think. You see...your finger is broken."

Following doctor's orders

A patient visited her doctor. "Doctor, it's been one month since my last visit, and I still feel miserable."

"Did you follow the instructions on the medicine I gave you?"

"Absolutely. The bottle specifically said, 'Keep tightly closed.'"

Quickies

What is an *eyedropper*? A clumsy ophthalmologist.

My mom just told me that she became an octogenarian on her last birthday. It's her life, so I guess she can do whatever she wants. I just hope she doesn't will them all her money.

Professional solution

My husband, a marriage counselor, often refuses to accompany me to parties and get-togethers. He says that so many people spoil his evening by asking him for advice. One day I saw my doctor, and I asked him if this ever happened to him. He told me that it happened to him all the time, but he had come up with a perfect solution.

"Oh?" I asked, thinking I could pass the advice on to my husband. "What do you do?"

"When someone starts talking about symptoms, I stop the conversation with one word—'Undress,'" the doctor explained with a smile.

The patient awakened after the operation to find herself in a room with all the blinds drawn.

"Why are all the blinds closed?" she asked the doctor.

"Well," the surgeon responded, "they're fighting a huge fire across the street, and we didn't want you to wake up and think the operation had failed."

Surprise

A woman went to a doctor's office. She was seen by one of the new doctors, but after about four minutes in the examination room, she burst out, screaming as she ran down the hall.

An older doctor stopped and asked her what the problem was, and she explained. He had her sit down and relax in another room.

The older doctor marched back to the first and demanded, "What is the matter with you? Ms. Terry is sixty-three years old, she has four grown children and seven grandchildren, and you told her she was *pregnant?*"

The new doctor smiled smugly and answered, "Cured her hiccups though, didn't I?"

Giddyap

"Doctor," Esther begs the psychiatrist, "you've got to help my husband. He thinks he's a racehorse. He wants to live in a stable; he walks on all fours; he eats hay!"

"I'm sure I can help him, but it will cost a lot of money."

"Money is no object—he's already won two races."

Good News/Bad News

After his examination, his doctor took Dan into the room and said, "Dan, I have some good news and some bad news."

Dan said, "Give me the good news first."

"They're going to name a disease after you."

Checkup

An older man went to the doctor for a checkup. During the after-checkup consultation, the doctor gave the old man some really good news: "You're in great shape for a sixty-year-old man."

The old man looked at the doctor and asked, "Who said I'm sixty years old?"

Surprised, the doctor asked, "You're not sixty? How old are you?"

"I'll turn eighty next month," the old man proudly stated.

"Gosh!" exclaimed the doctor. "I'm always curious about genetics. Do you mind if I ask you at what age your father died?"

"Who said my father is dead?" asked the patient.

"You mean he's not dead?" exclaimed the doctor.

"Nope," stated the old man. "He'll be one hundred and four this year."

"With such a good family medical history, your grandfather must have been pretty old when he died."

Again the old man asked, "Who says my grandfather is dead?"

"He's not dead?!"

"Nope, he'll be one hundred and twenty-nine this year, and he's getting married next week."

"Why at his age would he want to get married?" exclaimed the doctor.

"Who says he wants to?"

Virus

A man returned to the United States from a trip overseas. Not feeling very well, he went directly to the hospital from the airport. After a barrage of extensive, expensive tests, he woke up to find himself in a private room.

The bedside phone rang. He picked it up and heard, "This is your doctor. We have discovered that you have an extremely contagious virus, so we have placed you in total isolation. We're putting you on a diet of pizzas, pancakes, and pita bread."

"Will that cure me?" the patient asked hopefully.

The doctor replied, "Well, no, but it's the only food we can get under the door."

Cured

Two psychiatrists were at a convention. As they conversed over a cup of coffee, one asked, "What was your most difficult case?"

The other replied, "I had a patient who lived in a pure fantasy world. He believed that an uncle in South America was going to die and leave him a fortune. All day long he waited for a letter to arrive from an attorney. He never went out; he never did anything. He merely sat around and waited for this fantasy letter from this fantasy uncle. I worked with this man for eight years. It was an eight-year struggle. Every day for eight years I worked, but I finally cured him, and then that stupid letter arrived!"

Medical terms and alternate meanings

- *Barium*: What doctors do when patients die
- *Cauterize*: Make eye contact with her
- *Dilate*: To live longer
- *GI series*: World Series of military baseball
- *Medical staff*: A doctor's cane
- *Morbid*: A higher offer than I bid
- *Nitrates*: Cheaper than day rates
- *Node*: Was aware of
- *Outpatient*: A person who has fainted
- *Pelvis*: Second cousin to Elvis
- *Recovery room*: Place to do upholstery
- *Terminal illness*: Getting sick at the bus station
- *Tumor*: More than once
- *Varicose*: Near by/close by
- *Vein*: Conceited

Practical purposes

"I think this will be your last visit," the analyst suggested.

"Does that mean I'm cured?" the patient asked.

"For all practical purposes, yes. I think we can safely say that your kleptomania is under control."

"That's terrific, doc. I wish I could do something to repay you for helping me."

"You've paid my fee," answered the doctor. "That's payment enough."

"I know," insisted the patient, "but isn't there some personal favor I could do for you?"

"Well," the doctor hesitated, "I'll tell you what. If you ever suffer a relapse, my son could use a nice portable color television."

A veterinarian was feeling ill and went to see his doctor. The doctor was asking all the usual questions—about symptoms, how long they had been occurring, etc.—when the vet interrupted him: "Hey, look, I'm a vet—I don't need to ask my patients these kinds of questions. I can tell what's wrong just by looking." He smugly added, "Why can't you?"

The doctor nodded, stood back, looked the patient up and down, quickly wrote out a prescription, handed it to him, and said, "There you are. Of course, if that doesn't work, we'll have to put you to sleep."

DOCTOR: Well, your leg is swollen, but I wouldn't worry about it.

PATIENT: No, and if your leg was swollen, I wouldn't worry about it either!

MAKING PLANS

Early one morning, my husband, who works in a funeral home, woke me, complaining of severe abdominal pains. We rushed to the emergency room, where they gave him a series of tests to determine the source of the pain.

My husband decided not to have me call in sick for him until we knew what was wrong. When the results came back, the nurse informed us that, true to our suspicions, he was suffering from a kidney stone.

I turned to my husband and asked, "Would you like me to call the funeral home now?"

With an alarmed look, the nurse quickly said, "Ma'am, he's not that sick!"

Q: "Do you recall the time that you examined the body?"

A: "The autopsy started around 8:30 p.m."

Q: "And Mr. Dennington was dead at the time?"

A: "No, he was sitting on the table wondering why I was doing an autopsy."

A recent article in the *Tulsa World* told about a laughing seminar being conducted at St. Francis Hospital. Conducted by medical doctors and psychiatrists, the seminar was to inform health professionals of recent medical research that shows the astounding health benefits of laughter. Laughter releases positive, healing endorphins from the brain that impact both mental and physical health. According to the article, recent research has shown that laughter will lower blood pressure, stabilize heart rate, and provide all the health benefits of physical exercise. The seminar was encouraging health professionals to find ways to get their patients to laugh in order to accelerate the healing process.

Solomon wrote over two thousand years ago, "A merry heart doeth good like a medicine" (Prov. 17:22). Nehemiah said, "The joy of the LORD is your strength" (Neh. 8:10). In the parable of the sower, the seed that fell on stony ground represented the person who received the Word with joy, but later tribulation and persecution robbed that person of their joy, and they dried up and shriveled away.

Don't let Satan steal your joy! You have reason to rejoice today with joy unspeakable and full of glory (1 Pet. 1:8). Jesus is seated at the right hand of God with all authority in heaven and on the earth. He is on your side. Nothing in your life has caught Him by surprise. He has sent you His Holy Spirit to guide you through life and make you an overcomer! So go ahead and rejoice in the Lord today!

eight

OUR FOUR-LEGGED FRIENDS

Man's Best Friend

A man brought a very limp dog into the veterinary clinic. As he laid the dog on the table, Doctor Buck pulled out his stethoscope, placing the receptor on the dog's chest. After a moment or two, the doc shook his head sadly and said, "I'm sorry, but your dog has passed away."

"What?" screamed the man. "How can you tell? You haven't done any testing on him or anything. I want another opinion!"

With that, the doc turned and left the room. In a few moments, he returned with a Labrador retriever. The retriever went right to work, sniffing the poor dog on the table and checking him out thoroughly. After a considerable amount of sniffing, the retriever shook his head sadly and said, "Woof."

The veterinarian then took the Labrador out and returned in a few moments with a cat, which walked around the poor dog several times and then sadly shook his head and said, "Meow." Then the cat jumped off the table and ran out of the room.

The veterinarian said, "There's nothing more I can do." He handed the man a bill for $600.

The dog's owner said, "That's outrageous! Six hundred dollars just to tell me my dog is dead?"

The doc shook his head sadly and explained, "If you had taken my word for it, the cost would have been $50, but with the Lab work and the cat scan...$600!"

Bad dog

At the end of the workday, an officer parked his police van in front of the station. His K-9 partner in the back of the van began barking.

A little boy standing nearby asked, "Is that a dog you got back there?"

"Yes," answered the policeman.

The little boy looked puzzled as he asked, "What'd he do?"

Less common sense

Two inexperienced hunters bought a bird dog. They took the dog out to give it a try. After a long while one man said to the other, "Well, we'll throw him up in the air one more time. If he still doesn't fly, I guess we'll have to return him."

Answering the question

A man walked into a bar and sat down next to a man with a dog at his feet. "Does your dog bite?" he asked.

"No," said the man.

A few minutes later the dog took a bite of the man's leg.

"Hey! I thought you said your dog doesn't bite."

"That's not my dog," replied the man.

The new dog

An avid duck hunter was in the market for a new bird dog. His search ended when he found a dog that could actually walk on water to retrieve a duck. Shocked by his find, he was sure none of his friends would ever believe him. He decided to try to break the news to a friend of his, a pessimist by nature, and invited him to hunt with him and his new dog.

As they waited by the shore, a flock of ducks flew by. They fired, and a duck fell. The dog responded and jumped into the water. The dog, however, did not sink, but instead walked across the water to retrieve the bird,

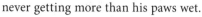 never getting more than his paws wet.

The friend saw everything but did not say a single word.

On the drive home, the hunter asked his friend, "Did you notice anything unusual about my dog?"

"Yeah," responded his friend. "Your dog can't swim.

The answer

During a countywide drive to round up all unlicensed dogs, a patrolman signaled a car to pull over. When the driver asked why he had been stopped, the officer pointed to the dog sitting on the seat beside him and asked, "Does your dog have a license?"

"No," the man said. "He doesn't need one."

"Yes, he does," answered the policeman.

"But," said the confused young driver, "I do all the driving."

Another dog-in-the-bar story

A guy walked into a bar with a small dog. "Get out of here with that dog!" yelled the bartender.

"But," insisted the guy, "this just isn't any dog. This dog can play the piano!"

"OK," sighed the bartender. "If he can play that piano, you both can stay…and drink on the house."

The dog starts playing ragtime, and the bartender and patrons were happily enjoying the music. Suddenly in came a bigger dog that grabbed the small dog by the scruff of the neck and dragged him out.

"What was that?!" asked the bartender.

"Oh, that was his mother. She wanted him to be a doctor."

A man tried to sell his neighbor his dog. "This is a talking dog," he said, "and you can have him for five dollars."

The neighbor said, "Who do you think you're kidding with this talking dog stuff? There ain't no such animal."

Suddenly the dog looked up with tears in his eyes, "Please buy me, sir," he pleaded. "This man is cruel. He never feeds me, bathes me, or takes me for a walk. And I used to be the richest trick dog in America. I performed before kings. Why, I was in the army and decorated ten times."

"Hey!" said the neighbor. "He can talk. Why do you want to sell him for just five dollars?"

"Because," said the seller, "I'm getting tired of all his lies."

Hiding his feelings

An easterner walked into a Western saloon and saw a dog sitting at a table playing poker with three men. He asked, "Can that dog really play cards?"

One of the men answered, "Yeah, but he's not much of a player. Whenever he gets a good hand, he wags his tail."

Talking canine

A man had a talking dog. He brought it to a talent scout. "This dog can speak English," he claimed.

"OK, Sport," the owner said to the dog. "What's on the top of a house?"

"Roof!" said the dog.

"Oh, come on" the talent agent responds. "All dogs go 'roof.'"

"No, wait," the guy continued. The he asked the dog, "What does sandpaper feel like?"

"Rough!" the dog answered.

The talent agent gives a condescending blank stare.

"No, hang on," the guy said. "This one will amaze you."

He turned to the dog and asked, "Who was the greatest baseball player of all time?"

"Ruth!" the dog responded.

The talent scout, having seen enough, booted them out of his office onto the street.

The dog turned to the guy and said, "Maybe I shoulda said DiMaggio?"

Following orders

A very spiritual couple felt it important to own an equally spiritual pet. So they went shopping. At a kennel specializing in a particular breed, they found a dog they liked quite a lot. When they asked the dog to fetch the Bible, he did it in a flash. When they instructed him to look up Psalm 23, he complied equally fast, using his paws with dexterity. They were impressed, purchased the animal, and went home.

That night they invited friends over to see their new pet. They were so proud of their new dog and his skills they couldn't wait to show him off. So as soon as their guests showed up, they called out their dog and put him through his tricks.

The guests were quite amazed. One of them asked, "Can he do any of the 'normal' dog tricks?"

"Well, we never thought about that," answered the husband. "Let's try one."

He turned to the dog and clearly pronounced the command, "Heel!"

Quick as a wink, the dog jumped up, put his paw on the man's forehead, closed his eyes in concentration, and bowed his head.

Mike kept telling the teacher that his dog ate his homework. We didn't believe him until his dog graduated from Yale.

All God's Critters

Did you know that dolphins are so intelligent that within only a few weeks of captivity, they can train people to stand at the very edge of the pool and throw them fish?

Confession

A man went to the confessional. "Forgive me, Father, for I have sinned."

"What is your sin, my son?" the priest asked.

"Well," the man started, "I used some horrible language this week, and I feel absolutely terrible."

"When did you use this awful language?" asked the priest.

"I was golfing and hit an incredible drive that looked like it was going to go over 250 yards, but it struck a power line that was hanging over the fairway and fell straight down to the ground after going only about a hundred yards."

"Is that when you swore?"

"No, Father. After that, a squirrel ran out of the bushes and grabbed my ball in his mouth and began to run away."

"Is that when you swore?"

"Well, no. You see, as the squirrel was running, an eagle came down out of the sky, grabbed the squirrel in his talons, and flew away!"

"Is *that* when you swore?" asked the amazed priest.

"No, not yet. As the eagle carried the squirrel away in his claws, it flew toward the green. And as it passed over a bit of forest near the green, the squirrel dropped my ball."

"Did you swear then?"

"No, because as the ball fell it struck a tree, bounced through some bushes, careened off a big rock, and rolled through a sand trap onto the green and stopped within six inches of the hole."

The priest sighed, "You missed the putt, didn't you?"

Gender miscommunications

A man was driving up a steep, narrow mountain road. A woman was driving down the same road in the opposite direction. As they passed each other, the woman leaned out the window and yelled, "Pig!"

The man immediately leaned out his window and replied with "Hog!"

They each continued on their way. As the man rounded the next corner, he hit a pig in the middle of the road.

Putting down the truth

Sign seen in a veterinarian's office: "All children left unattended will be given a free kitten."

Q: What do reindeer have that no other animals on earth have?

A: Baby reindeer.

Shocked

Some racehorses were staying in a stable. During the lazy afternoon, they began talking about their racing records.

One of them began to boast about his track record. "I've won eight of my last sixteen races!"

Another horse said, "Well, I've won twenty out of my last twenty-seven races!"

"Oh, that's good, but out of my last thirty-seven races, I've won thirty-two!" bragged yet another horse.

At this point, they noticed that a greyhound had been listening.

"I don't mean to boast," said the greyhound, "but I've been listening to your records. I have to say that I've won eighty-nine out of my last ninety-one races!"

The horses were clearly amazed.

"Wowwwww!" said one after a hushed silence. "A talking dog!"

Short stories

A rancher asked a veterinarian for some free advice. "I have a horse that walks normally sometimes, and sometimes he limps. What shall I do?"

The veterinarian replied, "The next time he walks normally, sell him."

Safe?

A young man was driving along on a country road on the way to see his girlfriend. As he passed a field filled with beautiful wildflowers, the idea struck him to stop and pick a bouquet of flowers. He pulled over on the side of the road and scooted under a fence.

He had barely begun romping through the field when he became aware of a rather mean-looking bull not far away, with head lowered and an evil look in his eye. The young man quickly looked around for an easy way out or for some help.

Far away, leaning comfortably on the fence, stood an old farmer taking in the situation but keeping quiet.

The young man called out to him, "Hey, Mister! Is that bull over there safe?"

To which the farmer shouted back, "Safe as can be, son. I can't say the same about you, though."

One solution

A man went to the board of health and complained, "I've got three brothers. We all live in one room. One of my brothers has six cats, another has five dogs, and the other has a goat. The smell is terrible. Can you do anything about it?"

The man thought about it and then asked, "Well, why don't you open the windows?" asked the man.

"What?" exclaimed the complainer to the health employee, "And lose all my pigeons?"

Smart sheriff

A farmer lived on a quiet, rural highway. But as time went by, the traffic slowly built up at an alarming rate. The traffic was so heavy and so fast that his chickens were being run over at a rate of three to six per day. So one day he called the sheriff's office and said, "You've got to do something about all these people driving so fast and killing all my chickens."

"What do you want me to do?" asked the sheriff.

"I don't care. Just do something about those drivers!"

The next day, the sheriff sent the county workers out to put up a sign that said, "Slow: School Crossing."

Three days later the farmer called the sheriff and said, "You've got to do something about those drivers. The school crossing sign seems to make them go faster."

So, again, the sheriff sent out the county workers to put up a new sign: "Slow: Children at Play."

That really sped them up. So the farmer called and told the sheriff, "Your signs are doing no good. Is it all right for me to put up my own sign?"

The sheriff, also at his wit's end, answered, "Sure thing; put up your own sign."

Three weeks later, the sheriff decided to call the farmer. "How's the problem with those drivers? Did you put up your sign?"

"Oh, I sure did," answered the farmer. "And not one chicken has been killed since then."

So the sheriff decided to drive out to the farmer's house and check out the sign. Written in large yellow letters on a black sign: "Slow: Nudist Colony."

Quick question

Why don't seagulls fly over the bay? Because if they did, they would be called *bagels.*

Sure, you can lead a horse to water; most folks can... but if you can get him to float on his back, then you've really got something!

Why, Mom?

A mother and baby camel were talking one day when the baby camel asked, "Mom, I have a question. Why do I have these huge three-toed feet?"

The mother replied, "Well, son, when we trek across the desert, your toes will help you to stay on top of the soft sand."

"OK," said the son.

A few minutes later, the son asked, "Mom, I have another question. Why do I have these great long eyelashes?"

"They are there to keep the sand out of your eyes on the trips through the desert."

"Thanks, Mom," replied the son. After a short while, the son returned and asked, "Mom, here's one more question. Why do I have these great big humps on my back?"

The mother, now a little impatient with the boy, replied, "They are there to help us store water for our long treks across the desert so we can go without drinking for long periods."

"That's great, Mom! So, we have huge feet to stop us from sinking, long eyelashes to keep the sand out of our eyes, and these humps to store water. But, Mom..."

"Yes, son?" asked the mother.

"I have one last important question: Why are we in the San Diego Zoo?"

Sending aid

Betty, who is very independent, likes to feed the pigeons in the park. One day she brought with her a whole loaf of fresh bread just to feed her daily company. Little by little, pinch by pinch, she fed each pigeon with joy.

Then suddenly a man rained on Betty's parade by telling her that she shouldn't throw away good food on a bunch of pigeons that can find food anywhere when there are a lot of people starving in Africa.

Betty said, "Well, maybe, but I can't throw that far!"

Greenhorns

A New York family bought a ranch out West where they intended to raise cattle. Friends visited and asked if the ranch had a name. "Well," said the would-be cattleman, "I wanted to name it the Bar-J. My wife favored Suzy-Q, one son liked the Flying-W, and the other wanted the Lazy-Y. So we're calling it the Bar-J-Suzy-Q-Flying-W-Lazy-Y."

"But where are all your cattle?" the friends asked.

"None survived the branding."

Zoo story

A kangaroo kept getting out of his enclosure at the zoo. Knowing that he could hop high, the zoo officials put up a ten-foot fence.

However, the 'roo was out the next morning, just sauntering around the zoo. A twenty-foot fence was put up. Again he got out. When the fence was built forty feet high, a camel in the next enclosure asked the kangaroo, "How high do you think they'll go?" The kangaroo said, "About a thousand feet, unless somebody thinks to lock the gate at night!"

TEACHER: We can learn from the ants. Ants work very hard every day. The ant works all the time. And what happens in the end?

STUDENT: Somebody steps on him.

Two snakes were crawling along when one asked, "Are we poisonous?"

The other said, "Yes, we're rattlesnakes. Why?"

The first replied, "I just bit my tongue."

Trying to nail a duck

One day a duck walked into a convenience store at two o'clock. "Do you have any duck food?" the duck asked.

"No, we don't have any duck food," replied the clerk.

"OK, thanks anyway." And the duck walked out.

The next day at two o'clock, the duck walked in again. "Got any duck food?" he asked.

The clerk became a little annoyed, "No! We don't have any duck food."

"Fine," answered the duck and walked out.

The third day at two o'clock the duck walked in and asked the same question. The clerk lost his temper. "I've told you twice; we don't have duck food. We've never had duck food, and we never will have duck food. If you ask me again, I'll nail your feet to the floor."

The next day at two o'clock the duck walked in "Got any nails?"

"No," answered the clerk.

"Good. Got any duck food?"

The bear facts

Two men went bear hunting. While one stayed in the cabin, the other went out looking for a bear. He soon found a huge bear. He shot at it, but only wounded it.

The enraged bear charged toward him. He dropped his rifle and started running to the cabin as fast as he could. He ran pretty fast, but the bear was just a little faster and gained on him every step. Just as he reached the open cabin door, he tripped and fell flat. Too close behind to stop, the bear tripped over him and went rolling into the cabin.

The man jumped up, closed the cabin door, and yelled to his friend inside, "You skin this one while I go and get another."

A lady went into a pet shop. There was a parrot on his perch. She said, "Oh, I've always wanted a parrot. I'm going to buy it."

The man said, "Now lady, I'm just not sure you want that bird. He talks all right, but he curses and talks very ugly."

She said, "I can retrain him. I'm going to buy him."

Sure enough, one day he ripped out all the expletives you could imagine. She was so upset. "I'm giving you another chance. You say, 'Yes, ma'am,' when I correct you. OK?"

He forgot and spouted off again, so she put him in the freezer. Sometime later, she took him out, frost all over his feathers. He was rigid, his beak blue! When he thawed out, the owner said, "Now, don't talk like that anymore!"

The parrot said, "All I want to know is, what in the world did that turkey in there do?"

nine

LIGHTHEARTED AGING

THE OTHER SIDE OF THE HILL

Taking a pledge seriously

An older lady had always wanted to travel abroad. Now that she wasn't getting any younger, she decided to do so before she died. Until now she had never been out of the country, so she went in person to the passport office and asked how long it would take to get one issued.

"You must take the loyalty oath first," responded the passport clerk as he pulled some paperwork out of a drawer. "Raise your right hand, please."

The old gal raised her hand.

"Do you swear to defend the Constitution of the United States against all its enemies, foreign and domestic?" asked the clerk.

The little old lady's face paled and her voice trembled as she asked in a small voice, "All by myself?"

Food for thought

The ninety-two-year-old, petite, well-poised and proud mother-in-law of my best friend, who is fully dressed each morning by eight o'clock, with her hair fashionably coiffed and makeup perfectly applied even though she is legally blind, moved to a nursing home today. Her husband of seventy years recently passed away, making the move necessary.

Maurine Jones is the most lovely, gracious, dignified woman whom I have ever had the pleasure of meeting. While I have never aspired to attain her depth of wisdom, I do pray that I will learn from her vast experience.

After many hours of waiting patiently in the lobby of the nursing home, she smiled sweetly when told her room was ready. As she maneuvered her walker to the elevator, I provided a visual description of her tiny room, including the eyelet sheets that had been hung on her window. "I love it," she stated with the enthusiasm of an eight-year-old having just been presented with a new puppy.

"Mrs. Jones, you haven't seen the room…just wait."

"That doesn't have anything to do with it," she replied. "Happiness is something you decide on ahead of time. Whether I like my room or not

106

doesn't depend on how the furniture is arranged; it's how I arrange my mind. I already decided to love it.

"It's a decision I make every morning when I wake up. I have a choice: I can spend the day in bed recounting the difficulty I have with the parts of my body that no longer work, or get out of bed and be thankful for the ones that do. Each day is a gift, and as long as my eyes open, I'll focus on the new day and all the happy memories I've stored away—just for this time in my life.

"Old age is like a bank account—you withdraw from what you've put in. So, my advice to you would be to deposit a lot of happiness in the bank account of memories."

Advantages of aging

- Kidnappers are not very interested in you.
- People no longer view you as a hypochondriac.
- Your secrets are safe with your friends because they can't remember them either.
- Your supply of brain cells is finally down to a manageable number.
- No one expects you to run into a burning building.
- There's nothing left to learn the hard way.
- Your joints are more accurate than the National Weather Service.
- In a hostage situation, you are likely to be released first.

The Senility Prayer

God, grant me the senility to forget the people I never liked anyway, the good fortune to run into the ones that I do like, and the eyesight to tell the difference.

Now that I'm older (but refuse to grow up), here's what I've discovered:

1. I started out with nothing, and I still have most of it.
2. I finally have my head together; now my body is falling apart.
3. Funny, I don't remember being absent-minded.
4. Of all the things I've lost, I miss my mind the most.

5. If all is not lost, where is it?
6. It is easier to get older than it is to get wiser.
7. I wish the buck stopped here. I sure could use a few.
8. It's hard to make a comeback when you haven't been anywhere.
9. If God wanted me to touch my toes, He would have put them on my knees.
10. When I'm finally holding all the cards, why does everyone decide to play chess?
11. It's not hard to meet expenses...they're everywhere.
12. The only difference between a rut and a grave is the depth.
13. These days, I spend a lot of time thinking about the here-after...I go somewhere to get something and then wonder what I'm here after.

More infernal truths

Experience is a wonderful thing. It enables you to recognize a mistake when you make it again.

A hymnbook made for seniors

- "Precious Lord, Take My Hand and Help Me Up"
- "It Is Well With My Soul, but My Knees Hurt"
- "Just a Slower Walk With Thee"
- "Go Tell It on the Mountain, but Please Speak Up"
- "Nobody Knows the Trouble I Have Seeing"

Optimism

Miss Dale, a long-time client at my beauty salon, was about to celebrate her one-hundredth birthday, and I had promised her complimentary hair services when she reached the century mark. I was delighted when she came in to collect her gift. As I prepared for her permanent wave, we discussed the fact that she was exactly twice my age.

Miss Dale was silent for a moment and then said, "There's only one thing that concerns me. Whatever will I do when you get too old to do my hair?"

Silent revenge

A grizzled old man was eating in a truck stop when three motorcycle bullies walked in. The first walked up to the old man, pushed his cigarette into the man's pie, and then took a seat at the counter.

The second walked up to the old man, spat in the man's milk, and then he too took a seat at the counter. The third walked up to the old man, turned over the old man's plate, and then he took a seat at the counter.

Without a word of protest, the old man quietly left the diner.

One of the bikers said to the waitress, "*Humph*, not much of a man, was he?"

She replied, "Not much of a truck driver either. He just backed his big rig over three motorcycles."

Time goes by

Inside every older person there's a young person wondering what happened.

A woman held a hammer behind her back as she spoke to the mirror: "Mirror, mirror on the wall, take all the time you need to phrase your response."

Two questions

Jimmie, an eighty-year-old gentleman, retired to Florida after his wife of fifty-eight years passed away. He was quite alone in the world and longed for companionship. One day in a park, he spied what he considered to be a very pretty silver-haired lady sitting alone on a park bench. Getting his nerve up, he approached her and asked, "Pardon me, but may I sit here with you?"

The silver-haired Marcia looked up to see a distinguished-looking, white-haired gentleman and replied, "Why, certainly."

For the next two hours the two talked about many topics and discovered that they had a great deal in common.

Finally, the old gentleman cleared his throat and asked sheepishly, "Marcia, may I ask you two questions?"

With great anticipation, Marcia replied, "Why, certainly!"

The old gentleman very gingerly got down on one knee, looked her in the eyes, and said, "Marcia, we've only known each other a few hours, but I feel we have a lot in common. Will you marry me?"

Marcia grabbed Jimmie's hands and said, "Why, yes, I will marry you!" and she kissed him gently on the cheek. "What was your other question?"

Jimmie scratched his neck and asked, "Will you help me get up?"

A gift

A travel agent looked up from his desk to see an older gentleman and lady peering in the shop window at the posters showing the glamorous destinations around the world. The agent had had a good week, and the dejected couple looking in the window gave him a rare feeling of generosity.

He called them into his shop. "I know that on your pension you could never hope to have a holiday, so I am sending you off to a fabulous resort at my expense, and I won't take no for an answer."

He took them inside and asked his secretary to write two flight tickets and book a room in a five-star hotel. They, as could be expected, gladly accepted and were off.

About a month later, the little elderly lady came into the travel agency.

"And how did you like your holiday?" asked the travel agent eagerly.

"The flight was exciting, and the room was lovely," responded the elderly lady. "I've come to thank you for such a wonderful experience. But one thing does puzzle me, and I just have to ask: 'Who was that old guy I had to share a room with?'"

A reporter asked a man on his ninety-fifth birthday, "To what do you credit your long life?"

The old-timer responded, "Well, I'm not sure yet. My lawyer's still negotiating with two breakfast cereal companies."

It worked

Aboard a flight to America, Grandma was taking her very first flight. They had only been aloft a few minutes when the old lady complained to the stewardess that her ears were popping.

The girl smiled and gave the older woman some chewing gum, assuring her that many people experienced the same discomfort.

When they landed in New York, Grandma thanked the stewardess. "Thank you, dear, the chewing gum worked fine," she said, "but tell me, how do I get it out of my ears?"

Hear some evil

Seems an elderly gentleman had serious hearing problems for a number of years. He finally went to the doctor to be fitted for some hearing aids. After some tests, the doctor was able to have him fitted for a set of hearing aids that allowed him to hear 100 percent.

The elderly gentleman went back in a month to the doctor, and the doctor said, "Your hearing is perfect. Your family must be really pleased you can hear again."

To which the gentleman said, "Oh, I haven't told my family yet. I just sit around and listen to the conversations. I've changed my will three times already!"

Son: Dad, are you growing taller all the time?

Dad: No, son. Why do you ask?

Son: Because the top of your head is poking up through your hair.

Parental thoughts

The people hardest to convince they're at the retirement age are children at bedtime.

Life lessons

It's frustrating when you finally know all the answers but nobody bothers to ask you the questions.

Aging and golfing

An eighty-year-old man's golf game was hampered by poor eyesight. He could still hit the ball well, but he couldn't see where it went. So a friend teamed him up with a ninety-year-old man who still had pretty good eyesight and was willing to serve as the younger man's spotter.

On the first tee, the younger man whacked the ball and turned to his older companion. "Can you see where that ball landed?"

"Yep," replied the ninety-year-old.

"Well, where did it go?"

"I don't remember," admitted the older man.

Senior citizen thoughts

- I'm very good at opening childproof caps with a hammer.
- I'm smiling all the time because I can't hear a word that you are saying.
- I'm sure they are making adults much younger these days.
- I'm wondering. If you're only as old as you feel, how could I still be alive at one hundred fifty?

- Eventually you will reach a point when you stop lying about your age and start bragging about it.
- Life's golden age is when the kids are too old to need babysitters and too young to borrow the car.

A reporter was interviewing a 104-year-old woman. "And what do you think is the best thing about being 104?" the reporter asked.

"Very little peer pressure," she responded with a smile.

Good answer

As paramedics, my partner and I were dispatched to check on a ninety-two-year-old man who had become disoriented. We decided to take him to the hospital for an evaluation. En route, with siren going, I questioned the man to determine his level of awareness.

Leaning close, I asked, "Sir, do you know what we're doing right now?"

He slowly looked up at me, then gazed out the ambulance window. "Oh," he replied, "I'd say about fifty, maybe fifty-five."

As one ages, it is important to remember which pocket has the pills and which pocket has the change. Yesterday I felt a heart pain and took three nickels.

Spunky

An old lady who lived on the third floor of a boarding house broke her leg. When the doctor put a cast on it, he warned her not to climb any stairs. Several months later, the doctor took off the cast.

"Can I climb stairs now?" asked the little old lady.

"Yes," the doctor replied.

"Thank goodness!" she said. "I'm sick and tired of shinnying up and down that drainpipe!"

A long life

The oldest inhabitant had celebrated his hundredth birthday, and the reporter of a local paper called on him for an interview. Having congratulated the old fellow, the reporter asked a few questions.

"To what do you attribute your longevity?" he inquired.

The centenarian paused a moment and then, holding up his hand and ticking the items off his fingers, began, "I never smoked, drank alcoholic liquors, or overate, and I always rise at six in the morning."

"But," protested the reporter, "I had an uncle who acted in that way, yet he only lived to be eighty. How do you account for that?"

"He didn't keep it up long enough," was the calm reply.

Gifts for Mom

Three sons were discussing the gifts they were able to give their elderly mother. The eldest said, "I built a big house for our mother."

The second said, "I sent her a Mercedes with a driver."

The youngest smiled and said, "I've got you both beat. You remember how Mom enjoyed reading the Bible? And you know she can't see very well. I sent her a remarkable parrot that recites the entire Bible. He's one of a kind. Mom just has to name the chapter and verse, and the parrot recites it."

Soon, Mom sent out her letter of thanks. To her first son: "The house you built is so huge. I live in only one room, but I have to clean the whole house."

To her second son: "I am too old to travel. I stay home most of the time. And the driver is rude!"

To her third son: "You have the good sense to know what your mother likes. The chicken was delicious."

Enough said

A grandmother was giving directions to her grown grandson who was coming to visit with his wife: "You come to the front door of the apartment complex. I am in apartment 14T. There is a big panel at the door. With your elbow, push button 14T. I will buzz you in. Come inside. The elevator is on the right. Get in, and with your elbow, hit 14. When you get out, I am on the left. With your elbow, hit my doorbell."

"Grandma, that sounds easy, but why am I hitting all these buttons with my elbows?" the grandson asked.

"You're surely not coming empty-handed, are you?"

A senior moment

Two elderly ladies had been friends for many decades. Over the years they had shared all kinds of activities and adventures. Through the years they had helped each other raise children, run a business, and bury their husbands. They had shared all the joys and sorrows of a full life.

Lately, their activities had been limited to meeting a few times a week to play cards and helping each other remember appointments.

One day they were playing cards when one looked at the other and said, "Now, don't get mad at me. I know we've been friends for a long time, but I just can't think of your name! I've thought and thought, but I can't remember it. Please tell me what your name is."

Her friend looked at her. For at least three minutes, she just stared and glared.

Finally she said, "How soon do you need to know?"

Quickies

Let's face it. Traveling just isn't as much fun when all the historical sites are younger than you are.

Careful

Two retired lady schoolteachers from Brooklyn, spending a year exploring western Canada, stopped at a small old-fashioned hotel in Alberta recently. One of the pair was inclined to be worrisome when traveling, and she couldn't rest until she had made a tour of the corridors to hunt out exits in case of fire. The first door she opened, unfortunately, turned out to be that of the public bath, occupied by an elderly gentleman taking a shower.

"Oh, excuse me!" the lady stammered, flustered. "I'm looking for the fire escape." Then she ran out.

To her dismay, she hadn't got far along the corridor when she heard a shout behind her and, looking around, saw the gentleman, wearing only a towel, running after her. "Where's the fire?" he yelled.

Daily quotes

"If you laugh a lot, when you get older, your wrinkles will be in the right places!"

The balding middle-aged man asked his barber, "Why do I have to pay full price for a haircut? There's so little of it."

"What you're paying for mostly is my time searching for it."

A tough old cowboy once counseled his grandson that if he wanted to live a long life, the secret was to sprinkle a little gunpowder on his oatmeal every morning.

The grandson did this religiously, and he lived to the age of ninety-nine!

When he died, he left fourteen children, twenty-eight grandchildren, thirty-five great-grandchildren, and a fifteen-foot hole in the wall of the crematorium.

OLD AGE REVISITED

- You know you're getting older when you bend over in the morning to tie your shoes and realize you didn't take them off the night before.
- I'm getting crow's feet around my eyes. And I tell you, that crow has big feet!

Positive attitude

Friends threw a big party down at the community center for a fellow on his ninety-ninth birthday. A young reporter was on hand to interview the honored guest for the local paper. After the interview was over, the reporter said, "I hope I'll be back next year to help you celebrate your centennial."

"Well, I don't see why not," replied the elderly gentleman. "You look healthy enough to me."

It's time for a hearing check

A ninety-two-year-old man went to the doctor for a physical. A few days later the doctor saw the man walking down the street with a gorgeous young lady on his arm. He smiled at his patient and walked on. The patient smiled back and went on around the block.

A couple of days later, the doctor talked to the man and said, "You're really doing great, aren't you?"

The old man replied, "Just doing what you said—'Get a hot mama and be cheerful.'"

The doctor paused and answered, "I didn't say that! I said, you've got a heart murmur. Be careful."

Grandmas

Two young boys were spending the night at their grandparents' house. At bedtime, the two boys knelt beside their beds to say their prayers when the younger one began praying at the top of his lungs, "I pray for a new bicycle. I pray for a new Nintendo. I pray for a new VCR."

His older brother leaned over and nudged the younger boy. "Why are you shouting your prayers? God isn't deaf."

To which the little brother replied, "No, but Gramma is!"

GRANDSON *(staring at his grandfather)*: Grandpa, were you on the ark when the Flood came?

GRANDPA: No, certainly not.

GRANDSON: Well, then, why weren't you drowned?

Too old

A pious man who had reached the age of one hundred five suddenly stopped going to church. Alarmed by the old fellow's absence, his pastor went to see him. The preacher asked, "How come, after all of these years, we don't see you at services anymore?"

The old man looked around and lowered his voice. "I'll tell you, preacher," he whispered. "When I got to be ninety, I expected God to take me any day. But then I got to be ninety-five, then one hundred, and then one hundred five. So I figured God is very busy and must've forgot about me, and I don't want to remind Him."

Crying man

When I went to lunch the other day, I noticed an elderly man about seventy-five or eighty years old sitting on a park bench near JCPenney, and he was sobbing his eyes out. I stopped and asked him what was wrong.

He said, "I have a twenty-two-year-old wife at home. She gets up every morning and makes me pancakes, sausage, fresh fruit, and freshly ground coffee."

"Well, then," I said, "why are you crying?"

"She also," he continued, "makes me homemade soup and brownies and loves me half the afternoon."

"Then, sir, why are you crying?"

"For dinner, she makes me a gourmet meal."

"But why are you crying?"

"I can't remember where I live!"

"Hey, Earl!"

"Hi, Clyde!"

"I can't remember where I parked my car."

"I know the feeling."

"You can't find your car either?"

"Nope, I'm trying to figure out if I drove here or walked."

Three elderly ladies who were hard of hearing were riding in a bus together. A couple of windows were open, and one of them said to another, "Windy, isn't it?"

One said, "No, it isn't Wednesday; it's Thursday!"

The third one said, "Yes, I'm thirsty too! Let's get off and have a Coke!"

You Know You're Getting Old When...

- You wonder why everyone is starting to mumble.
- You finally find something you've been looking for, for ages but can't remember WHY you wanted it.
- You can't finish a conversation because you don't remember what you were talking about.
- You can't be tried by a jury of your peers because there are none.
- Everyone is happy to give you a ride because they don't want you behind the wheel.
- A passing funeral procession pauses to see if you need a lift.
- You can remember seeing double-feature movies for a nickel, some with sound.

- You're sitting on a park bench, and a Boy Scout comes up and helps you cross your legs.
- It takes a couple of tries to get over a speed bump.
- You run out of breath walking down a flight of stairs.
- Your children begin looking middle-aged.
- You walk with your head high, trying to get used to your bifocals.
- You burn the midnight oil until 9:00 p.m.
- Your little black book contains names ending in MD.
- You stoop to tie your shoes and wonder what else you can do while you're down there.
- In the morning you hear snap, crackle, pop, and it isn't your breakfast cereal.

GROWING OLD TOGETHER

An eighty-year-old couple was worried because they kept forgetting things all the time. The doctor assured them there was nothing seriously wrong except old age, and suggested they carry a notebook and write things down so they wouldn't forget. Several days later the old man got up to go to the kitchen. His wife said, "Dear, get me a bowl of ice cream while you're up."

"OK," he said.

"…and put some chocolate syrup on it and a few cherries on it, too." Then she added, "You'd better write all this down."

"I won't forget," he said. Twenty minutes later he came back into the room and handed her a plate of scrambled eggs and bacon.

She glared at him. "Now, I told you to write it down! I knew you'd forget."

"What did I forget?" he asked.

She replied, "My toast!"

There it goes again!

While on a car trip, an elderly couple stopped at a roadside restaurant for lunch. After finishing their meal, the elderly woman left her glasses on the table, but she didn't miss them until they were back on the highway. By then, they had to travel quite a distance before they could find a place to turn around.

The elderly man fussed and complained all the way back to the restaurant.

When they finally arrived at the restaurant, as the woman got out of the car to retrieve her glasses, the man yelled to her, "While you're in there, you might as well get my hat too!"

Len's obituary

Len died, so his wife Lila went to the local paper to put a notice in the obituaries. The gentleman at the counter, after offering his condolences, asked Lila what she would like to say about her husband of thirty-five years.

Lila replied, "Oh, just put, 'Len died.'"

The gentleman, somewhat perplexed, said, "That's it? Just, 'Len died?' Surely there must be something more you'd like to say about Len. If it's money you're concerned about, the first five words are free. We really should say something more."

So Lila pondered for a few moments and finally said, "OK, then. You can put, 'Len died. Boat for sale.'"

A little old couple walked into McDonald's one cold winter night. They looked out of place, as there were a lot of young couples and families eating there that night. Some of the customers looked at them admiringly, and you could tell what they were thinking: "Look, there is a couple who has been through a lot together, probably sixty or more years."

The little old man walked up to the cash register and placed his order for one hamburger, one order of french fries, and one drink. The little old man unwrapped the plain hamburger and carefully cut it in half. He placed one half in front of his wife. Then he counted the french fries, dividing them into two piles, and neatly placed one pile in front of his wife. He took a sip of the drink; his wife took a sip and then set the cup down between them.

As the man began to eat his few bites of hamburger, the crowd began to get restless. Again, you could tell what they were thinking: "That poor old couple. All they can afford is one meal for the two of them."

As the man began to eat his french fries, one young man came over to the old couple's table. He politely offered to buy another meal for the old couple to eat. The old man replied that they were just fine—they were used to sharing everything.

The crowd noticed that the little old lady hadn't eaten a bite. She just sat there watching her husband eat and occasionally taking turns sipping the drink. Again, the young man came over and offered to buy them something to eat.

This time the lady explained that no, they were used to sharing everything together. As the little old man finished eating and was wiping his face neatly with the napkin, the young man could stand it no longer. Again, he came over to their table and offered to buy some food. After being politely refused again he finally asked a question of the little old lady: "Ma'am, why aren't you eating? You said that you share everything. What is it that you are waiting for?"

She answered, "The teeth!"

Memory

An old gentleman, confined to a nursing home, was walking down the hallway when he noticed Mrs. Barnstone sitting in a chair in the lounge. He walked up to her and asked her to guess his age.

"Give me a kiss, and I'll tell you."

So the old gentleman kissed her. "You're eighty-eight," answered Mrs. Barnstone.

"Why, yes! How did you know?"

"You told me at breakfast."

Dealing With Dying

Cemetery

Two men were walking home after a party and decided to take a shortcut through the cemetery just for laughs. Right in the middle of the cemetery, they were startled by a tap-tapping noise coming from the misty shadows. Trembling with fear, they found an old man with a hammer and chisel, chipping away at one of the headstones.

"Mister," one of them said, after catching his breath, "you scared us half to death—we thought you were a ghost! What are you doing working here so late at night?"

"They misspelled my name!"

Fun quotes

"When I die, I want to die like my grandfather who died peacefully in his sleep—not screaming like all the passengers in his car."

Old age is when former classmates are so gray and wrinkled and bald they don't recognize you.

Final request

A woman from New York prepared her will and made her final arrangements. As part of these arrangements, she met with her minister to talk about what type of funeral service she wanted. She told him she had two final requests: first, she wanted to be cremated; second, she wanted her ashes to be scattered over Bloomingdale's.

"Why Bloomingdale's?"

"That way I know my daughters will visit me twice a week."

ten

PURSE STRING MUSINGS

WHO HOLDS THE PURSE STRINGS?

A farmer robbed a bank and went to prison. He received a letter from his wife that said: "Here you are in jail, smoking cigarettes from the state, eating their food, and having a good time. I'm at home alone, so who's going to plow the fields so that I can plant the potatoes?"

He wrote her back, saying, "Don't plow the field; that's where I buried the money!"

She wrote a note back and said, "Someone must be reading your mail! The sheriff and his men came out yesterday and plowed every inch of the field! What should I do now?"

He wrote back and said, "Now plant the potatoes."

There was a man who had worked all of his life and was a real miser when it came to his money. He loved money more than anything, and just before he died, he said to his wife, "Now listen. When I die, I want you to take all my money and put it in the casket with me, because I want to take my money to the afterlife with me."

And so he got his wife to promise him with all of her heart that when he died, she would put all of the money in the casket with him. One day he died. He was stretched out in the casket, the wife was sitting there in black, and her friend was sitting next to her.

When they finished the ceremony, just before the undertakers got ready to close the casket, the wife said, "Wait just a minute!"

She had a box with her. She came over with the box and put it in the casket. Then the undertakers locked the casket down and rolled it away. Her friend said, "Girl, I know you weren't foolish enough to put all that money in there with that man."

She said, "Listen, I'm a Christian; I can't lie. I promised him that I was going to put his money in that casket with him, and that's what I did."

Her friend was amazed, "You mean to tell me you put all his money in the casket with him?"

"I sure did," said the wife. "I wrote him a check."

The last of the big spenders

A man and a woman walked into a very posh Main Street furrier. "Show the lady your finest mink!" the fellow said. So the owner of the shop showed them an absolutely gorgeous full-length coat.

As the lady tried it on, the furrier discreetly whispered to the man, "Ah, sir, that particular fur goes for $65,000."

"No problem! I'll write you a check."

"Very good, sir," said the shop owner. "Today is Saturday. You may come by on Monday to pick it up after the check has cleared."

So the man and the woman left.

On Monday, the fellow returned. The storeowner was outraged. "How dare you show your face in here? There wasn't a single penny in your checking account!"

"I just had to come by," grinned the guy, "to thank you for the most wonderful weekend of my life!"

Surprise performance

A lady threw a party for her granddaughter and went all out—a caterer, a band, and a hired clown. Just before the party started, two homeless men showed up looking for a handout.

Feeling sorry for them, the woman told them that she would give them a meal if they would help chop some wood for her out back. Gratefully, they headed to the rear of the house.

The guests arrived, and all was going well. But then the clown called to report that he was stuck in traffic and would probably not make the party at all.

The woman was very disappointed and unsuccessfully tried to entertain the children herself. She happened to look out the window and saw one of the hired men doing cartwheels across the lawn. She watched in awe as he swung from tree branches, did midair flips, and leaped high in the air.

She spoke to the other man and said, "What your friend is doing is absolutely marvelous. I have never seen such a thing. Do you think your friend would consider repeating this performance for the children at the party today? I would pay him $100!"

The other fellow said, "Well, I dunno. Let me ask him.

"Hey, Willie! For $100, would you chop off another toe?"

Reading the will

A lawyer was reading the will of a rich man to the people mentioned in the will: "To my loving wife, Rose, who stood by me in the rough times as well as the good—the house and $2 million.

"To my daughter, Jessica, who looked after me in illness and kept the business going—the yacht, the business, and $1 million.

"And to my cousin, Dan, who hated me, argued with me, and thought I would not remember him in my will—you were wrong. Hello, Dan!"

———————

A woman came home, screeched her car into the driveway, ran into the house, and shouted at the top of her lungs: "Fred, pack your bags, I won the lottery!"

Fred said, "That's great. What should I pack—beach stuff or mountain stuff?"

The wife yelled back, "It doesn't matter…just get out!"

Fatherly advice

The junior Murray had become involved in a financial tangle. In a moment of weakness he had loaned a friend $500 without getting a receipt.

Then the young man found that he needed his money back. In desperation, he consulted his father. The father said, "Oh, that's easy, son. Write him and say you need the $1,000 you loaned him."

The young Murray said, "You mean $500."

"I do not," said the father. "You say $1,000, and he will immediately write back that he owes you only $500. Then you have it in writing."

Nothing ventured

The girl was very rich, and the young man was poor but honest. She liked him, but that was all, and he knew it. One night he had been a little more tender than usual. "You are very rich," he ventured.

"Yes," she replied frankly. "I am worth $1,250,000."

"And I am poor."

"Yes."

"Will you marry me?"

"No."

"I thought you wouldn't."

"Then why did you ask me?"

"Oh, just to see how a man feels when he loses $1,250,000."

———————

The young lady told her friend that she was going to marry a rather eccentric millionaire.

"But," her friend said, "everyone thinks he's a little bit cracked."

"He may be cracked," the young lady said, "but he certainly isn't broke."

A success story

An up-and-coming yuppie finally established a software firm in Columbia, Maryland. A friend asked him how he managed to "stick it out" during the lean startup period.

"It was easy," replied the new entrepreneur. "I just rolled up my sleeves, worked longer and harder, then borrowed a hundred thousand dollars from my parents."

$$$$

A one-dollar bill met a twenty-dollar bill. "Hey, where have you been? I haven't seen you around here much."

The twenty answered, "I've been hanging out at the casinos, went on a cruise, back to the U.S. for a while, went to a couple of baseball games, to the mall, out to eat, over to the mountains, the beach...that kind of stuff. How about you?"

To this the one-dollar bill replied with a sigh, "Oh, you know, same old stuff...church, church, church."

WHAT WE'LL DO FOR A BUCK!

Fighting fire

One dark night outside a small town, a fire started inside the local chemical plant. Before long it exploded into flames, and an alarm went out to fire departments for miles around. After fighting the fire for over an hour, the chemical company president approached the fire chief and said, "All of our secret formulas are in the vault in the center of the plant.

They must be saved! I will give $50,000 to the engine company that brings them out safely!"

As soon as the chief heard this, he ordered the firemen to strengthen their attack on the blaze. After two more hours of attacking the fire, the president of the company offered $100,000 to the engine company that could bring out the company's secret files.

From the distance a long siren was heard, and another fire truck came into sight. It was a local volunteer fire company composed entirely of men over sixty-five. To everyone's amazement, the little fire engine raced through the chemical plant gates and drove straight into the middle of the inferno. In the distance, the other firemen watched as the old timers hopped off their rig and began to fight the fire with an effort that no one had ever seen before. After an hour of intense fighting, the volunteer company had extinguished the fire and saved the secret formulas.

Joyously the chemical company president announced that he would double the reward to $200,000 and walked over to thank each of the volunteers personally.

After thanking each of the old men individually, the president asked the group what they intended to do with the reward money.

The fire-truck driver looked him right in the eye and said, "The first thing we're going to do is fix the brakes on that truck!"

Smart advertising

A man traveling in southern Oklahoma was heading toward Texas. He saw a sign reading, "Last chance for $1.25 gas." So even though he still had a quarter tank, he stopped to fill up.

As he was paying for his gas, he asked the clerk, "How much is gas in Texas?"

The clerk answered, "$1.10."

Advertising

A bank opened a branch near a cemetery. In the window the president put a sign that read, "You can't take it with you when you go, but here's a chance to be near it!"

More of the same

A millionaire was walking into the building he owned when a man came over and said, "Mr. Bronson, you probably don't remember me, but twenty years ago—on this very spot—I asked you for ten dollars, and you gave me ten dollars. I've never forgotten that."

"Ah, the goodness of mankind," smiled Mr. Bronson. "And now you've come to pay me back."

"Not exactly," said the man frankly. "I was just wondering if you've got another ten."

This and that

When a person's outgo exceeds his income, his upkeep may be his downfall.

Advice

The coed came running in tears to her father, "Dad, you gave me some bad advice!"

"I did? What?"

"You told me to put my money in that big bank, and now that big bank is in trouble!"

"What makes you say that?" asked her confused father.

"They just returned one of my checks with a note saying, 'Insufficient Funds.'"

Having money can't buy everything, but then again neither can having no money.

Money can't buy happiness, but it can help you look for it more quickly in a convertible.

I decided to stop worrying about my teenage daughter's driving and take advantage of it. I got one of those bumper stickers that say, "How's my driving?" and put a 900 number on it. At fifty cents a call, I've been making thirty-eight dollars a week.

Bumper sticker

"I've taken a vow of poverty. To annoy me, send money."

CREDIT MANAGER: Do you have any money in the bank?

LOAN APPLICANT: Certainly.

CREDIT MANAGER: How much?

LOAN APPLICANT: I don't know. I haven't shaken it lately.

I received some bad news today. You know the money you get from those ATM machines? All that money comes from your account!

A woman was telling her friend, "It is I who made my husband a millionaire."

"And what was he before you married him?" asked the friend.

The woman replied, "A billionaire."

One friend said to the other, "Look, we've been friends for a long time. I know what you're losing on the market. Tell me, this has to affect your sleep. How do you sleep at night?"

The other person says, "Like a baby."

"What do you mean?"

"I wake up every two hours and cry my eyes out!"

THE BUSINESS OF MONEY

World famous

An American tourist in Tel Aviv was about to enter the impressive Mann Auditorium to take in a concert by the Israel Philharmonic. He was admiring the unique architecture, the sweeping lines of the entrance, and the modern décor throughout the building. Finally he turned to his escort and asked if the building was named for Thomas Mann, the world-famous author.

"No," his escort said, "it's named for Frederic Mann, from Philadelphia."

"Really? I have never heard of him. What did he write?"

"A check."

You get what you pay for

A man took his place in the theater, but his seat was too far from the stage. He gestured to the usher and told him, "This is a mystery, and I have to watch a mystery up close. Get me a better seat, and I'll give you a handsome tip."

So the usher moved him to the second row, and the man handed him a quarter. The usher looked at the quarter and then leaned over and whispered, "The wife did it."

Just following directions

The manager of a hotel, finding that a guest had departed without paying his hotel bill, wrote him: "My dear Mr. Smythe, please send the amount of your bill as soon as possible."

To this, Mr. Smythe wrote politely: "My dear Mr. Manager, the amount of my bill was one hundred and ten dollars. Yours, respectfully."

A window salesman phoned a customer. "Hello, Mr. Brown," said the sales rep. "I'm calling because our company replaced all the windows in your house with our triple-glazed, weather-tight windows more than a year ago, and you still haven't sent a single payment."

The customer replied, "But you said they would pay for themselves in twelve months."

The story of wealth

A young man asked an old rich man how he had made his money. The old guy fingered his worsted wool vest and said, "Well, son, it was 1932, depth of the Great Depression. I was down to my last nickel. I invested that nickel in an apple. I spent the entire day polishing the apple, and at the end of the day, I sold the apple for ten cents. The next morning, I invested those ten cents in two apples. I spent the entire day polishing them and sold them at 5:00 p.m. for twenty cents. I continued this system for a month. By the end of that month, I'd accumulated a fortune of $1.37."

The old man paused, cleaned his glasses, put them back on, and looked the young man straight in the eyes. "Then my wife's father died and left us two million dollars."

What a heart

The staff at a local United Way office realized that it had never received a donation from one of the town's most successful businessmen. The person in charge of contributions called him to persuade him to contribute, "Our research shows that out of a yearly income of at least one million dollars, you give not a penny to charity. Wouldn't you like to give back to the community in some way?"

The businessman mulled this over for a moment and replied, "First, did your research also show my mother is dying after a long illness and has medical bills that are several times her annual income?"

Embarrassed, the United Way representative quietly mumbled, "Um...no."

"Or," the businessman continued, "that my brother, a disabled veteran, is blind and confined to a wheelchair?"

The stricken United Way representative began to stammer out an apology but was interrupted when the businessman added, "Or that my sister's husband died in a traffic accident—leaving her penniless with three children?"

The humiliated United Way representative simply said, "I had no idea."

The businessman cut him off, "So, if I don't give any money to them, why should I give any to you?"

Practical business

A customer sent an order to a distributor for a large amount of goods totaling a great deal of money.

The distributor noticed that the previous bill hadn't been paid. The collections manager sent a voicemail for them saying, "We can't ship your new order until you pay for the last one."

The next day the collections manager received a fax from the customer: "Please cancel the order. We can't wait that long."

A shrewd businessman

A gentleman walked into a bank in New York City and asked for the loan officer. He said he was going to Europe on business for two weeks and needed to borrow $5,000.

The bank officer answered that the bank would need some kind of security for such a loan, but that the bank would be happy to consider the loan. So the gentleman handed over the keys to a new Rolls Royce parked on the street in front of the bank.

Everything checked out, and the bank agreed to accept the car as collateral for the loan. An employee drove the Rolls into the bank's underground parking and parked it there.

Two weeks later, the gentleman returned, repaid the $5,000 and the interest, which came to $15.41. The loan officer said, "We are very happy to have had your business, and this transaction has worked out very nicely. But we are a little puzzled. While you were away, we checked you out and found that you are a multimillionaire. What puzzles us is why would you bother to borrow $5,000? You obviously don't need to borrow such money."

The gentleman replied, "Where else in New York can I park my car safely for two weeks for fifteen bucks?"

Money Vices

A clean little Johnny joke

Little Johnny's father wanted to cure his son of gambling. He asked the boy's principal for help.

The next day the principal called the boy's father. "I think I have cured your son of gambling," he said.

"How did you do it?" asked Johnny's father.

"Well, he looked at my beard and said, 'Sir, is that beard real or false? I wouldn't mind betting five dollars that it is false.'

"'All right,' I replied. 'I'll take your bet. Now pull it and see.' Of course, my beard is real," said the principal. "He had to pay me five dollars, so I'm sure that will cure him of gambling."

"Oh, no!" groaned the father. "Last night he bet me ten dollars that you'd let him pull your beard!"

eleven

SMILING AT THE LAW

PECULIAR LAWS

Did you know it is against the law to let a monkey smoke a cigarette in Indiana?

———————

It is also against the law in Pennsylvania for a man to put an ice cream cone in his hip pocket.

Love conquers all

My Uncle George likes to drive sports cars—unfortunately not always with the owner's permission. Anyway, he was serving some time in prison—again—when the nicest thing happened to him. He married the warden's daughter.

The warden didn't mind so much that his daughter married my Uncle George, but he was a little upset that they eloped.

INTERPRETING THE LAW

Insanity plea

The district attorney stared at the jury in disbelief. Bitterly he asked, "What possible excuse could you have for acquitting this man?"

The foreman answered, "Insanity."

The district attorney quickly asked, "All twelve of you?"

Gaining freedom

A prison warden had an unusual manner for determining afternoon passes. He would call the eligible prisoners in one at a time and ask them two questions. If they correctly answered both, they could gain an afternoon pass.

He called in the first prisoner and asked, "What would happen to you if I were to poke out one of your eyes?"

"I would be half blind, of course," answered the prisoner.

"What would happen," continued the warden, "if I poked out the other eye?"

"I would be completely blind," answered the prisoner.

The warden wrote him an afternoon pass. As the prisoner left, he whispered the correct answers to the next eligible prisoner.

The warden called the second prisoner in and asked him, "What would happen if I cut off one of your ears?"

The second prisoner answered, "I would be blind in one eye."

Confused the warden asked a second question, "What would happen if I cut off your other ear?"

"I would be completely blind," answered the second prisoner.

"Can you explain your answers?" asked the warden.

"Sure," smiled the second prisoner. "My hat would fall down over my eyes."

The warden wrote the pass.

Clever lawyer

The popular mayor, the revered football coach, and a successful attorney were playing poker one evening in the back of the small-town cafe. In walked the sheriff who raided their game and hauled them off before the local judge.

After listening to the sheriff's story, the judge sternly asked the mayor, "Were you gambling, Mayor?"

"Oh, no! No, Your Honor, I was not gambling," answered the mayor.

"Well, if you say so, I've got to believe you. Dismissed!"

Then he turned to the coach. "Were you gambling, Coach?"

"No, Your Honor, I was not," replied the successful coach.

"Well, if you say so, I've got to believe you. Do well in the regionals Friday night. Dismissed."

Turning to the lawyer, the judge said, "You were gambling. No use to deny it."

The lawyer looked the judge coolly in the eye and replied, "With whom?"

Speeding ticket

Two highway patrolmen stopped a man for speeding on the state highway in Waxahachie, Texas. As they were writing up the ticket, one cop turned to the other and said, "How do you spell Waxahachie?"

The other admitted, "I don't know."

So the first one said, "What are we going to do? If we spell it wrong, it will get dismissed."

The second cop said, "Why don't we just let him go and stop him again when he gets to Waco?"

A highway patrolman stopped a man and said, "I've got to give you a ticket. Your taillights are out."

The man said, "Oh, how terrible."

The highway patrolman said, "Now, settle down. It's not that bad. You can get it fixed."

The man said, "You don't understand. I want to know what happened to my $60,000 boat I was pulling!"

Explaining the obvious

A truck driver was driving along on the freeway when he saw a sign, "Low bridge ahead." Before he knew it, the bridge was right ahead of him, and he got stuck under it. Cars were backed up for miles. Finally, a police car came up. The policeman got out of his car and said, "Got stuck, huh?"

The truck driver replied, "No, I was delivering this bridge and ran out of gas."

Pleading

The judge looked sternly at the two men in his court and asked, "Can't this case be settled out of court?"

One of the men looked up at the judge and said, "Your Honor, we were trying to do that when the police came."

Eager beaver

A rookie police officer was assigned to ride in a cruiser with an experienced partner. A call came over the car's radio telling them to disperse some people who were loitering.

The officers drove to the street and observed a small crowd standing on a corner. The rookie rolled down his window and said, "Let's get off the corner."

No one moved, so he barked again, "Let's get off the corner!"

Intimidated, the group of people began to leave, casting puzzled glances in his direction. Proud of his first official act, the young policeman turned to his partner and asked, "Well, how did I do?"

"Pretty good," replied the veteran, "especially since that was a bus stop."

Railroad crossing

In a terrible accident at a railroad crossing, a train smashed into a car and pushed it nearly four hundred yards down the track. Though no one was killed, the driver took the train company to court.

At the trial, the engineer insisted that he had given the driver ample warning by waving his lantern back and forth for nearly a minute. He even stood and convincingly demonstrated how he'd done it. The court believed his story, and the suit was dismissed.

"Congratulations," his lawyer said to the engineer when it was over. "You did superbly under cross-examination."

"Thanks," he said, "but he sure had me worried."

"How's that?" the lawyer asked.

"I was afraid he was going to ask if the lantern was lit!"

Recently a poll of people in New York City showed that 80 percent of them wouldn't want to live anywhere else in the world. Besides, it was reported, it would violate the terms of their parole.

Repeat performance

One night, a lady stumbled into the police station with a black eye. She claimed she heard a noise in her backyard and went to investigate. The next thing she knew, she was hit in the eye and knocked out cold.

An officer was sent to her house to investigate, and he returned a half hour later with a black eye as well.

"What happened? Did you get hit by the same person?" asked his captain.

"No, sir," he replied, "but I did step on the same rake."

Winning the job

A soldier was asked to report to headquarters for assignment. The sergeant said, "We have a critical shortage of typists. I'll give you a little test. Type this," he ordered, giving him a pamphlet to type and a sheet of paper, and pointing to a desk across the room that held a typewriter and an adding machine.

The soldier, quite reluctant to become a clerk-typist, made a point of typing very slowly, and he made sure that his work contained as many errors as possible. After the soldier finished, he handed the typed paper to the sergeant who barely glanced at it. "That's fine. Report for work tomorrow at 8:00."

"But aren't you going to check the test?" asked the soldier.

The sergeant grinned. "You passed the test before you started typing—when you sat down at the typewriter instead of at the adding machine."

Well, you asked

A politician asked his friend, a professor of philosophy, for some advice on presenting interesting speeches. The professor suggested, "You should start with a question like, 'Why are we all here?'"

The politician tried out the idea before various audiences, and it went well. Well, that is, until he somehow got persuaded to speak to the inmates of a mental health clinic.

He began his usual way, "Why are we all here?"

Quick as a flash came back a reply from a voice in the audience, "Because we aren't all there."

A mother's lament

One mother was complaining to another. "Kids these days are so fickle. My daughter has changed majors three times this year!"

"I didn't know she was in college," said her friend.

"She's not. She's in the army!"

Not using the head

The police were sure the criminal was inside the movie theater. The chief told the sergeant to surround the building and have all the exits watched. An hour later, the sergeant returned with his men. "He got away," he told the chief.

"Got away!" the chief roared. "Did you guard all the exits like I told you?"

"Sure."

"Then how did he get away?"

"Don't know. Maybe he used one of the entrances."

Knowing the future

BENNY: My grandpa knew the exact day of the year and the exact time of day that he was going to die. He was right about that too.
LOUIE: Wow, that's incredible. How did he know all of that?
BENNY: A judge told him.

Following the law

Two good old boys were driving a truck through the back roads of West Virginia when they came to an overpass with a sign that read, "Clearance 11'3"."

They got out and measured their rig, which was 12'4". "What do you think?" asked one as they climbed back into the cab.

The driver looked to his left, then to his right, and checked the rear-view mirror. "Not a cop in sight. Let's take a chance."

A faxful of stories

The prosecuting attorney approached the witness. "Do you happen to know any of the people you see in the jury box?"

The witness looked them over and thought carefully before replying. "Yes, I know over half of them."

"Keep in mind the oath you have made before this court," continued the attorney. "Can you swear that you know more than half of them?"

"Why, I certainly can!" fired back the witness. "In fact, I think I know more than all of them put together!"

———

At the conclusion of the trial, the jury found the defendant not guilty. The defendant was so happy that he hugged his lawyer. His lawyer congratulated him and handed him a bill.

The happy defendant looked at the bill and gulped. "This says I have to pay ten thousand dollars now and five hundred a month for five years! It sounds like I'm buying a Mercedes-Benz!"

The lawyer smiled, "You are."

Carjacking foiled

An elderly woman did her shopping and upon return found four males in her car. She dropped her shopping bags and drew her handgun, proceeding to scream at them at the top of her voice that she knows how to use it and that she will if required…so get out of the car.

The four men didn't wait around for a second invitation to get out and ran like mad, while the lady proceeded to load her shopping bags into the back of the car and get into the driver's seat.

Small problem, however—her keys wouldn't fit in the ignition.

Her car, identical to the car she first approached, was parked four spaces further down. So she moved her bags into her own car and drove to the police station. The sergeant she told her story to nearly split his sides with laughter and pointed to the other end of the counter where four very nervous males were reporting a carjacking by a mad, elderly woman. No charges were filed.

Thanks, I think

Since he was a Texan being tried in New York, the young man felt he didn't have a prayer in beating the murder rap. Thus, shortly before the jury was to retire, he bribed one of the jurors to find him guilty of manslaughter, not murder.

The jury was out for days, after which they returned a verdict of manslaughter. Cornering the bribed juror, the Texan whispered, "Thanks a million. How did you manage it?"

"It wasn't easy," admitted the bribed juror. "All the others wanted to acquit you."

Better rephrase that

At the police station, Bubba explained to the police officer why his cousin shot him. "Well," Bubba began, "we was havin' a good time drinking when my cousin Ray picked up his shotgun and said, 'Hey, do ya fellows wanna go hunting?'"

"And then what happened?" the officer interrupted.

"From what I remember," Bubba said, "I stood up and said, 'I'm game.'"

Running out of excuses

A police officer pulled over a guy who had been weaving in and out of the lanes. He walked up to the guy's window and said, "Sir, I need you to blow into this breathalyzer tube."

The man responded, "Sorry, officer, I can't do that. I am an asthmatic. If I do that, I'll have a really bad asthma attack."

"OK. I need you to come down to the station to give a blood sample."

"I can't do that, either. I am a hemophiliac. If I do that, I'll bleed to death."

"Well, then, we need a urine sample," insisted the police officer.

"Sorry. I am also a diabetic. If I do that, I'll get really low blood sugar."

"All right. Then I need you to come out here and walk this white line," added the officer.

"I can't do that, officer."

"Why not?" asked the exasperated officer.

"Because I'm drunk."

Sad truth

A reporter had done a story on gender roles in Kuwait several years before the Gulf War, and she noted then that women customarily walked about ten feet behind their husbands.

She returned to Kuwait recently and observed that the men now walked several yards behind their wives. She approached one of the women for an explanation. "This is marvelous," she said. "What enabled women here to achieve this reversal of roles?"

The Kuwaiti woman sadly replied, "Land mines."

Mistaken identity

A drunk phoned the police to report that thieves had been in his car. "They've stolen the dashboard, the steering wheel, the brake pedal, even the accelerator!" he shouted.

The police were dumbfounded and dispatched an officer to the scene. However, before the police arrived, the phone rang a second time with the same voice on the line. "Never mind," he said with a hiccup. "I got in the back seat by mistake."

Success

The police recently busted a man selling "secret formula" tablets he claimed gave eternal youth. When going through their files, the police noticed that the same man had been charged with the same criminal medical fraud four previous times: in 1794, 1856, 1928, and 1983.

Correction

A dictator was in his office alone when his bodyguards heard a loud explosion inside his office. Rushing in, they saw him on the floor, face bloodied, and they asked, "What happened, Mr. Chairman?"

"A letter bomb," whispered the dictator.

"But a letter bomb would have wounded your hands, not your mouth," replied one of his experienced men.

"But I was sealing it," explained the dictator.

The kindness of a stranger

A man came out of a shopping mall to find that the side of his parked car was rammed in. He began to get upset but was relieved to see a note under the windshield wiper.

He took the note and began to read: "As I'm writing this, about a dozen people are watching me. They think I'm giving you my name, phone number, and insurance company. But I'm not."

Sweet revenge

A woman was charged with a traffic violation. When asked for her occupation, she said she was a schoolteacher. The judge rose from the bench. "Madam, I have waited years for a schoolteacher to appear before this court." He smiled with delight. "Now sit down at that table and write, 'I will not pass through a red light' five hundred times."

Huh?

The Baltimore Police Department, famous for its superior K-9 unit, was somewhat taken aback by a recent incident. Returning home from work, a young worker had been shocked to find her house ransacked and burglarized. She telephoned the police at once and reported the crime.

The police dispatcher broadcast the call on the channels, and a K-9 unit patrolling nearby was the first on the scene.

As the K-9 officer approached the house with his dog on a leash, the woman ran out on the porch, clapped a hand to her head, and moaned, "I come home from work to find all my possessions stolen. I call the police for help, and what do they do? They send a blind policeman!"

A police officer pulled over a pickup truck from out of state on Highway 51. He said to the driver, "Got any ID?"

The driver said, "'Bout what?"

Fishing with a license

A couple of young boys were fishing at their favorite spot when the game warden jumped out of the bushes. One boy threw down his rod and took off through the woods with the warden hot on his heels.

After running half a mile, the boy stopped to catch his breath, and the game warden snagged him.

"Let me see a license, boy!" snapped the warden as he impatiently waited for the boy to dig through his wallet.

The boy pulled out his wallet and showed the warden his fishing license.

"Well, son," said the warden, "you must be dumber than a box of rocks! You don't have to run from me—you have a valid license!"

"Well, I do," said the boy, "but the guy back there doesn't."

A police car pulled up in front of Grandma Betty's house, and Grandpa Benny got out. The polite policeman explained that this elderly gentleman said that he was lost in the park and couldn't find his way home.

"Oh, Benny," said Grandma, "you've been going to that park for thirty years! How could you get lost?"

Leaning close to Grandma so the policeman couldn't hear, Benny whispered, "I wasn't lost... I was just too tired to walk home."

Keeping track

A beautiful blonde was visiting Washington DC. This was her first time to the city, so she wanted to see the Capitol building. Unfortunately, she couldn't find it, so she asked a police officer for directions. "Excuse me, officer," the girl said. "How do I get to the Capitol building?"

The officer said, "Wait here at this bus stop for the number 54 bus. It'll take you right there."

She thanked the officer, and he drove off.

Three hours later the police officer came back to the same area and, sure enough, the girl was still waiting at the same bus stop. The officer got out of his car and said, "Excuse me, but to get to the Capitol building I said to wait here for the number 54 bus. That was three hours ago. Why are you still waiting?"

The girl said, "Don't worry, officer. It won't be long now. The 45th bus just went by!"

Criminal comments

The judge said to the defendant, "I thought I told you I never wanted to see you in here again."

"Your Honor," the criminal said, "that's what I tried to tell the police, but they wouldn't listen."

One too many questions

At a meeting in an iron curtain country, one of the party members, Comrade B, got up and said, "Comrade leader, I have only three questions to ask: 'If we are the greatest industrial nation, what happened to our cars? If we have the best agriculture, what happened to our bread? If we are the finest cattle raisers, what happened to our meat?'"

The presiding chairman stared at Comrade B and replied, "It is too late to reply tonight. At our next meeting I will answer your questions fully."

When the meeting opened the following week, another party member rose and said, "I have just one question: What happened to Comrade B?"

A policeman at a train station noticed a lady bowed over the steering wheel of her car in discomfort. He walked over and asked if she was all right.

Half crying and half laughing, the woman said, "For ten years I've driven my husband to catch his train. This morning I forgot him!"

The sneeze

They walked in tandem, each of the ninety-three students filing into the already crowded auditorium. With rich maroon gowns flowing and wearing the traditional caps, they looked almost as grown up as they felt.

Dads swallowed hard behind broad smiles, and moms freely brushed away tears.

This class would not pray during the commencement—not by choice but because of a recent court ruling prohibiting it. The principal and several students were careful to stay within the guidelines allowed by the ruling. They gave inspirational and challenging speeches, but no one mentioned divine guidance, and no one asked for blessings on the graduates or their families.

The speeches were nice, but they were routine until the final speech received a standing ovation.

 A solitary student walked proudly to the microphone. He stood still and silent for just a moment, and then he delivered his speech...an astounding sneeze!

The rest of the students rose immediately to their feet, and in unison they said, "God bless you!"

The audience exploded into applause. The graduating class had found a unique way to invoke God's blessing on their future with or without the court's approval.

PRESIDENT: Is our advertising getting results?

VICE PRESIDENT: It sure is! Last week we advertised for a night watchman, and the next night we got robbed!

LIFE IN THE MILITARY

Quick thinking

A new army recruit was given guard duty at 2:00 a.m. He did his best for a while, but about 4:00 a.m. he couldn't fight it and went to sleep. He awakened to find the officer of the day standing before him. Remembering the heavy penalty for being asleep on guard duty, this smart young man kept his head bowed for another moment.

Then he looked upward and reverently said, "A-a-men!"

War progress

A large group of enemy soldiers was moving down a road when they heard a voice call from behind a huge boulder, "One U.S. Marine is better than ten enemy soldiers."

The enemy soldiers' commander quickly ordered ten of his best men around the boulder, whereupon a gun battle broke out and continued for several minutes. Then complete silence reigned.

The voice again called out, "One U.S. Marine is better than one hundred enemy soldiers."

Furious, the commander of the enemy soldiers sent his next best hundred troops around the boulder, and instantly a huge gunfight began.

After ten minutes of battle, again silence.

The voice called out again, "One U.S. Marine is better than one thousand enemy soldiers." The enraged enemy commander mustered one thousand fighters and sent them to the other side of the boulder.

Rifle fire, machine gun, grenades, and cannon fire rang out as a terrible battle was fought... then silence.

Eventually one wounded enemy fighter crawled out from behind the boulder. He struggled over to his commander and, with his dying words, told his commander, "Don't send any more men... it's a trap. There's two of them."

Military matters

As we stood in formation at the Pensacola Naval Air Station, our flight instructor said, "All right! All you idiots fall out."

As the rest of the squad wandered away, I remained at attention. The instructor walked over, stood eye to eye with me, and raised a single eyebrow.

I smiled and said, "Sure was a lot of 'em!"

Rifle range

At one army base, the annual trip to the rifle range had been canceled for the second year in a row, but the semiannual physical fitness test was still on as scheduled.

One soldier mused, "Does it bother anyone else that the army doesn't seem to care how well we can shoot, but they are extremely interested in how fast we can run?"

Going for help

A number of new air force recruits were being taken on their first training flight. The plane had just leveled out after taking off when one of the engines locked up and another began smoking badly.

Adjusting his parachute, the instructor strove for nonchalance as he made his way to the hatch door. "Now I want you men to keep perfectly calm," he said, "while I go for help."

Pilot

The chief of staff of the U.S. Army decided that he would intervene in the recruiting crisis affecting all armed services. He directed an air force base to be opened and that all eligible young men and women be invited for a tour. As he and his staff were standing near a new M-1 battle tank, twin brothers who were well built and neatly dressed walked up. The two of them looked as if they had just stepped out of a recruiting poster. The chief of staff walked up to them, stuck out his hand, and introduced himself. He looked at the first young man, "Son, what skills can you bring to the best army in the world?"

The young man looked at him and said, "I'm a pilot."

The general excitedly turned to his aide and said, "Get him in today! See to it!"

He then turned to the second young man and asked, "What skills can you bring to the best army in the world?"

The young man replied, "I chop wood!"

"Son, we don't need wood choppers in the army of the twenty-first century. What else can you do?"

"I don't understand. You hired my brother!"

"Of course we did," explained the general. "He's a pilot."

The young man rolled his eyes. "Well, I have to chop it before he can pile it!"

The exact truth

An army private was filling out a questionnaire for a bank loan and had to answer the question: "How long has your present employer been in business?"

He thought for a minute, then wrote, "Since 1776."

Advice

A young, freshly minted lieutenant was sent to Bosnia as part of the peacekeeping mission. During a briefing on land mines, the captain asked for questions.

Our intrepid soldier raised his hand and asked, "If we do happen to step on a mine, sir, what do we do?"

"Normal procedure is to jump two hundred feet in the air and scatter oneself over a wide area."

The draftee was awakened roughly by his platoon sergeant after the rookie's first night in the army barracks. "It's four-thirty!" roared the sergeant.

"Four-thirty!" gasped the recruit. "Man, you'd better get to bed. We've got a big day tomorrow!"

Bragging

Down at the veteran's hospital, a trio of old-timers ran out of tales of their own heroic exploits and started bragging about their ancestors. Each vet wanted to top the other.

"My great-grandfather, at age thirteen," one declared proudly, "was a drummer boy at Shiloh."

"Mine," boasted another, "went down with Custer at the Battle of Little Big Horn."

"I'm the only soldier in my family," confessed vet number three, "but if my great-grandfather were living today, he'd be the most famous man in the world."

"What'd he do?" his friends wanted to know.

Taking his time, the vet finally answered, "Nothing much. But he would be 165 years old."

Mind reader

A general and a colonel were walking down the street. They met many privates, and each time the colonel would salute he would mutter, "The same to you."

The general's curiosity soon got the better of him, and he asked, "Why do you always say that?"

The colonel answered, "I was once a private, and I know what they're thinking."

Traction

During an army war game, a commanding officer's jeep got stuck in the mud. The CO saw some men lounging around nearby and asked them to help him get unstuck.

"Sorry, sir," said one of the loafers, "but we've been classified dead, and the umpire said we couldn't contribute in any way."

The CO stared at them awhile and then turned to his driver and said, "Go drag a couple of those dead bodies over here and throw them under the wheels to give us some traction."

Wrong again

During training exercises, a lieutenant driving down a muddy back road encountered another car stuck in the mud with a red-faced colonel at the wheel. "Your jeep stuck, sir?" asked the lieutenant as he pulled alongside.

"Nope," replied the colonel, coming over and handing him the keys, "Yours is."

WAR ON YOU

"Hello, Mr. President. This is Paddy down in County Cavan, Ireland. I'm ringing to inform you that we are declaring war on your nation."

"Well, Paddy, this is news. How big is your army?"

"*Hmm*, there is myself, my cousin Sean, my next door neighbor Gerry, and the dominoes team from the pub—that makes eight."

"Well," the president sighed, "I have one million men at my command."

"Begorra! I'll call you back."

The next day Paddy does indeed call back. "Mr. President, the war is still on. We have managed to acquire some equipment. We have two common harvesters, a bulldozer, and Murphy's tractor."

Again the president sighed. "But I have sixteen thousand tanks and fourteen thousand armored personnel carriers."

"Really! I'll call you back."

The next day Paddy called back, "We have managed to get ourselves airborne with Ted's ultra-light with a couple of rifles in the cockpit."

"But Paddy, I have ten thousand bombers, twenty thousand MiG-19 attack planes, and now I have two million men."

"I'll call you back."

The next day Paddy called the president back and canceled the war.

"I'm sorry to hear that," said the president. "Why?"

"We've decided there's no way we can feed two million prisoners."

THE LAW OF TAXES

Questions

An IRS agent was interviewing a farmer. During the interview, the agent asked, "How much would you say your prize bull is worth?"

The farmer scratched his chin and answered, "Well, that depends—for tax purposes or has he been hit by a train?"

Short ones

A taxpayer received a strongly worded "second notice" that his taxes were overdue.

Hastening to the collector's office, he paid his bill, saying apologetically that he had overlooked the first notice.

"Oh," confided the collector with a smile, "we don't send out first notices. We have found that the second notices are more effective."

Relief

A nervous taxpayer was talking with the IRS tax auditor who had come to review his records. At one point, the auditor exclaimed, "Mr. Carr, we feel it is a great privilege to be allowed to live and work in the USA. As a citizen, you have an obligation to pay taxes, and we expect you to eagerly pay them with a smile."

"Thank goodness," returned the taxpayer with a giant grin on his face. "I thought you were going to want me to pay cash."

Politics

Long ago there was a presidential election that was too close to call. No compromise or solution could be determined, so finally the two political parties decided to settle the election with an ice-fishing contest. The candidate who caught the most fish in three days would be declared the winner.

So the two candidates, Paul and Bob, were sent to Wisconsin in the dead of winter. At the end of the first day, Paul returned with ten fish. Bob, however, showed up with none. After the second day, Paul came back with ten more fish. Again, Bob showed up with none.

That night, Bill came into Bob's cabin with some savvy political advice. "I think, Bob, you need to find out what's going on. Tomorrow morning you need to spy on Paul to see if he's cheating."

At the end of the third day, Paul returned with fifty fish. Bob crept up to Bill and whispered, "You were right. He's cheating! He's cutting holes in the ice!"

Trying to please Mama

The first woman was elected U.S. president. She called her mom to make sure she was coming to the inauguration.

"I don't know, dear. What would I wear?"

"Don't worry, Mom. I'll send a designer to help you."

"But you know I need special foods for my diet."

"Mom, I'm going to be president. I can get you the food you need."

"But how will I get there?"

"I'll send a limo, Mom. Just come!"

"OK, OK, if it makes you happy."

The great day came, and Mama was seated with the future cabinet members. She nudged the man on her right. "See that girl, the one with her hand on the Bible? Her brother's a doctor!"

twelve

LIVING LIFE WITH A SMILE

Keeping Up With the Times

Changes in America

In a logic discussion group, the professor was trying to explain how society's ideals change with the time. "For example," he said, "take the 1921 Miss America. She stood 5 feet 1 inch tall, weighed 108 pounds, and had measurements of 30-25-32. How do you think she'd do in today's version of the contest?"

The class fell silent for a moment. Then one student piped up, "She would never have entered the contest today."

"Why is that?" asked the professor.

"For one thing," the student pointed out, "her grandchildren would never let her."

Interesting modern definitions

- *College*—the four-year period when parents are permitted access to the telephone.

- *Kissing*—a means of getting two people so close together that they can't see anything wrong with each other.

Groan

Back in the sixties when the economy was suffering in England, some consideration was given to selling the Rock of Gibraltar to the French. All negotiations were halted when the British learned the French were planning to rename it "De Gaulle Stone."

Workplace Laughter

He has spoken

Two men were down on their luck and decided to paint houses to earn some extra money. To start their business, they asked the minister of a local church if he would be interested in their services. He agreed, and the men went out to buy the paint.

As they drove to the paint store, they decided that they would mix half paint and half water to try to increase their profits. When they finished the job, they called the minister outside to look at their work.

"It looks wonderful," the minister said. As he started to hand them the check, a small rain cloud appeared. All at once, there was lightning and thunder, and the church area was drenched with rain. As the rain hit, the new church paint started running.

Suddenly the three of them stood there in disbelief as a voice from above roared, "Repaint! Repaint! And thin no more!"

What a sale

When the store manager returned from lunch, he noticed his clerk's hand was bandaged, but before he could ask about the bandage, the clerk spoke up, "Guess what! I finally sold that terrible, ugly suit we've had so long!"

"You mean that repulsive pink-and-blue double-breasted thing?"

"That's the one!"

"Great!" cried the manager. "But why is your hand bandaged?"

"Oh," the clerk replied, "after I sold that guy the suit, his guide dog bit me."

Plotting

One worker said to another, "How long have you been working here?"

He answered, "Since they threatened to fire me."

Service

Arnold and his wife were cleaning out the attic one day when he came across a ticket from the local shoe repair shop. The date stamped on the ticket showed it was over eleven years old. They both laughed and tried to remember which of them might have forgotten to pick up a pair of shoes over a decade ago.

"Do you think the shoes will still be in the shop?" Arnold asked.

"Not very likely," his wife said.

"It's worth a try," Arnold said, pocketing the ticket. He went downstairs, hopped into the car, and drove to the store.

With a straight face, the man said, "Just a minute. I'll have to look for these."

He disappeared into a dark corner at the back of the shop. Two minutes later, he called out, "Here they are!"

"No kidding!" Arnold called back. "That's terrific! Who would have thought they'd still be here after all this time."

The man came back to the counter, empty-handed. "They'll be ready Thursday," he said calmly.

Repeat performance

Carrying three pieces of luggage, a young lady walked up to the airport check-in counter and requested," I want the first piece to go to Cleveland, the second to go to Toronto, and this last piece of luggage to go to Florida."

The agent said, "I'm sorry, we can't do that."

The young lady swiftly replied, "Last month you did it."

I took a part-time job as an opinion poll sampler. On my first call, I said, "Hello, this is a telephone poll."

And the man replied, "Yeah, and this is a street lamp."

Employment found

A guy came home to his wife and said, "Guess what! I've found a great job. A 10:00 a.m. start, 2:00 p.m. finish, no overtime, no weekends, and it pays $800 a week!"

"That's great," his wife said.

"Yeah, I thought so too," he agreed. "You start Monday."

Looking in

A man had his first appointment with the psychiatrist, and when asked why he was there, the man said, "Doctor, I'm tired of being on the outside looking in."

"Well," responded the doctor, "sounds like we have to try to improve your self-image. Let's get a few basic facts first. What do you do for a living?"

The patient replied, "I'm a window washer."

Random thoughts

- Isn't it odd that the person with the strongest beliefs in hard work and dedication by employees is usually the boss?
- Money is not everything—there's American Express, MasterCard, and Visa.

The interview

"Well, sir," said the interviewer to the job applicant, "for a man with no retail experience, you are certainly asking for a high wage."

"Well," responded the applicant, "the work will be a lot harder for me since I won't know what I'm doing."

Following orders

My company posted a notice next to the time clock. It said that the company calendar had a typo, and that the union-won holiday wasn't really a holiday at all. The company blamed the printer for this mistake. The first line of the notice read, "Please Take Notice." So the guy standing next to me did!

Rethinking

A manager of a large office noticed a new man one day and told him to come into his office. "What's your name?" he asked the new guy.

"John," the new guy answered.

The manager scowled, "Look, I don't know what kind of a namby-pamby place you worked for before, but I don't call anyone by their first name. It breeds familiarity, and that leads to a breakdown in authority. I refer to my employees by their last name only—Smith, Jones, Baker—that's all. I am to be referred to only as Mr. Robertson. Do you understand?"

As the new man nodded, the manager continued, "Now that we got that straight, what's your last name?"

The new guy sighed, "Darling. My name is John Darling."

"OK, John. Now the next thing we need to discuss is…"

Cutting in line

A local department store was having a big sale. The publicity department had done a great job advertising, and on the morning of the sale a long line formed in front of the store waiting for the 8:30 a.m. opening. A small man pushed his way to the front of the line, only to be pushed back amid loud and colorful curses. On the man's second attempt, he was punched square in the jaw and knocked around a bit, and then thrown to the end of the line.

As he got up the second time, he said to the person at the end of the line, "That does it! If they hit me one more time, I don't open the store!"

Free enterprise

A city boy moved to the country and bought a mule from an old farmer. The farmer agreed to deliver the mule the next day.

The next day, the farmer drove up and said, "Sorry, but I have some bad news. The mule is dead."

"Well, then, just give me my money back."

"Can't do that. I went and spent it already."

"OK, then," said the city boy, "just unload the mule."

"What ya gonna do with him?"

"I'm going to raffle him off."

"You can't raffle off a dead mule!" protested the farmer.

"Sure I can. Just watch me. I just won't tell anybody he's dead."

A month later, the farmer met up with the city boy and asked, "Whatever happened with that dead mule?"

"I raffled him off. I sold a hundred tickets at two dollars apiece and made a ninety-eight dollar profit."

"Didn't anyone complain?"

"Just the guy who won. So I gave him the two dollars back."

That special word

The manager of a ladies' dress shop called in one of her clerks. "Jane, your figures are well below those of the other clerks."

"I'm sorry, ma'am," mumbled Jane. "Can you give me any advice on how to do better?"

"Well, there is an old trick that might help. Look through a dictionary until you come to a word that has a particular power for you. Memorize that word, and work it into your sales pitch."

Sure enough, Jane's sales figures went way up. At the end of the month, Jane explained. "It took me all weekend to find the right word, but I discovered *fantastic*. My first customer on Monday told me that her girl had been accepted to an exclusive prep school, so I said, 'Fantastic!' When she told me her daughter made As, I said 'Fantastic!' She then bought $800 worth of clothes. The second customer needed a new formal for her evening at the country club. I said, 'Fantastic,' and she bought a dress and hundreds of dollars worth of clothes for other events. It's been like that all week; the customers keep boasting; I keep saying, 'Fantastic,' and they keep buying."

"Excellent," said the manager. "By the way, what did you used to say to customers before you discovered your power word?"

Jane answered, "I used to say 'So what?'"

Rave

Years ago I once went for a job at an airline. The interviewer asked me why I wanted to be a stewardess. Quite honestly I told her it would be a great chance to meet men.

She looked at me and said, "But you can meet men anywhere."
I quickly answered, "Not strapped down."

Pat and Mike landed themselves a job at the sawmill. Just before morning break, Pat yelled, "Mike! Help! I've lost my finger!"

"Have you now," said Mike. "And how did you do it?"

Pat replied, "I just touched this big, shiny thing here like this...whoops! There goes another one!"

Too much

Reaching the end of a job interview, the human resources person asked a young engineer fresh out of MIT what kind of a salary he was looking for.

"In the neighborhood of $140,000 a year, depending on the benefits package."

"Well, what would you say to a package of five weeks vacation, fourteen paid holidays, full medical and dental, company matching retirement fund to 50 percent of salary, and a company car leased every two years...say, a red Corvette?" asked the interviewer.

"Wow! Are you kidding?" exclaimed the recruit.

"Yeah," admitted the interviewer, "but you started it."

Sales on top

Two bowling teams, one made up of accountants and one made up of salespeople, chartered a double-decker bus for a weekend bowling tournament in Atlantic City.

The accountants rode in the bottom of the bus. The salespeople rode on the top level. The team made up of accountants down below was having a great time when one of them realized that there was no noise coming from up above.

One of the accountants went up to investigate. When he got to the top, he found all the salespeople frozen in fear, staring straight ahead at the road, and clutching the seats in front of them with white knuckles.

He asked, "What's going on up here? We're having a great time down below."

One of the salespeople looked up and answered, "Yeah, but you've got a driver!"

Banking arrangements

A banker fell overboard from a friend's sailboat. He floundered in the water.

The friend grabbed a life preserver, held it up, not knowing if the banker could swim, and shouted, "Can you float alone?"

"Well, you would need some sort of collateral," the banker replied, "but this is a bad time to discuss business."

Boarding

At the airport for a business trip, I settled down to wait for the boarding announcement at Gate 35. Then I heard an announcement: "We apologize for the inconvenience, but Delta Flight 570 will board from Gate 41."

So I hurried over to Gate 41. Not ten minutes later, another announcement: "Delta Flight 570 is indeed boarding at Gate 35. Sorry for the inconvenience." So I hurried back to Gate 35.

Soon I again heard the public address system say, "Thank you for participating in Delta's physical fitness program."

Who's who?

A photographer for a national magazine was assigned to take pictures of a great forest fire. He was advised that a small plane would be waiting at a local airfield to fly him over the fire.

The photographer arrived at the airstrip just an hour before sundown.

Sure enough, a small Cessna airplane was waiting. He jumped in with his equipment and shouted, "Let's go!"

The tense man sitting in the pilot's seat swung the plane into the wind and soon they were in the air, though flying erratically.

"Fly over the north side of the fire," said the photographer, "and make several low-level passes until I tell you to stop."

"Why?" asked the nervous pilot.

"Because I'm going to take pictures!" yelled the photographer. "I'm a photographer, and photographers take pictures."

After a long pause, the "pilot" replied, "You mean you're not my flight instructor?"

Easy question

At the end of an exhausting road trip, a salesman pulled into his last motel. Because of the lateness of the hour, he left his luggage at the desk and went to the dining room to eat. After a leisurely dinner, he reclaimed his luggage and realized he had forgotten his room number.

"Excuse me," he spoke to the desk clerk. "Could you please tell me which room I'm in?"

"Certainly, sir," replied the desk clerk pleasantly. "You're in the lobby."

Traveling

A skycap, loaded down with suitcases, followed the couple, also loaded with luggage, to the airline check-in counter.

As they approached the line, the husband glanced at the pile of luggage and said to the wife, "Honey, why didn't you bring the piano too?"

"Are you trying to be funny?" she said.

"No," he sighed forlornly. "I think I left the tickets on it."

Whatever you say

Two attorneys went into a diner, sat down, and ordered two Cokes. Then they produced sandwiches from their briefcases and started to eat.

The owner became quite concerned, marched over to them, and told them, "You can't eat your own sandwiches in here!"

The attorneys looked at each other, shrugged their shoulders, and then exchanged sandwiches.

The right person

"In this job we need someone who is responsible," said the employer. "I hope you fit that description."

"Yes, sir, I'm your man," answered the potential employee. "On my last job, every time anything went wrong, they said I was responsible."

New on the job

Late one night during bad weather, the following was heard over the radio at an airport control tower:

HELICOPTER PILOT: Tower, I'm holding at 3000 over Heli-pad 1.

SECOND VOICE: NO! You can't be doing that! I'm holding at 3000 over that pad!

There was a brief moment of radio silence.

First voice began again, "Uh, tower, please ignore last message. That's just my new copilot on his first flight."

Pride

As one of the relatively few female airline pilots, I've often been mistaken for a flight attendant, ticket agent, or even snack bar employee.

Occasionally people who see me in uniform ask if I'm a real pilot. Still others congratulate me for making it in a male-dominated field.

One day, I was in the restroom before a flight. I was at the sink, brushing my teeth, when a woman walked through the door and looked over at me. "My sister would be so proud of you!" she remarked.

I figured her sister must be in the airline business, so I smiled and asked why.

Replied the woman, "She's a dentist."

Trading jobs

A cardiologist developed a new operating procedure that would cut down the time that heart surgery would take. He began to make more money lecturing on his new procedure than actually using the procedure. So he decided to lecture full-time. He hired a driver and purchased a limousine. After about six months of lecturing, his driver turned to him and said, "You know, this is not completely fair."

"What do you mean?"

"Well, you get paid $50,000 every time you do this lecture, and that's more than I get paid in a year," complained the driver.

The surgeon explained that the procedure was very complicated, and he and only he could explain it.

"That's not true. I've heard your lecture so often, I know I could deliver it just as well."

"OK. Let's see. You deliver this lecture."

So the driver and the surgeon traded places. The driver gave a wonderful presentation and answered many questions. Finally a member of the audience stood and asked a very complex question.

The driver responded, "You know, I have done this lecture 187 times, and I have never been asked such an easy question. As a matter of fact, that question is SO basic that I am going to let my driver answer it."

Watchman

A man got a job as a night watchman at a factory. The factory had been experiencing great losses lately, so the man was ordered to check the bags and pockets of the workers as they left. One evening one worker tried to leave the plant with a wheelbarrow full of newspapers. The night watchman was immediately suspicious.

"Hey, bud," he ordered. "Let me take a look at what's under all those papers." The night watchman diligently looked, but he found nothing but newspapers.

"You see," explained the worker, "I pick up all the extra newspapers in the lounges and take them to the recycle plant. That way I save a few trees and make a little money."

For the next few months, the worker left every night with a wheelbarrow full of newspapers, but the watchman remained alert and checked them every night.

One evening the night watchman got a summons to his supervisor's office. Without a word of explanation, the supervisor fired the night watchman.

"What! As long as I was on duty, absolutely nothing was stolen from this plant!"

"Oh, really?" said the supervisor. "Then how do you account for the fact that our recent audit shows that we have lost two hundred wheelbarrows?"

Tough teacher

A schoolteacher injured his back and had to wear a plaster cast around the upper part of his body. It fit under his shirt and was not noticeable at all. On the first day of the term, still with the cast under his shirt, he found himself assigned to the toughest students in the school.

Walking confidently into the rowdy classroom, he opened the window as wide as possible and then busied himself with desk work. When a strong breeze made his tie flap, he took the desk stapler and stapled the tie to his chest.

He had no trouble with unruly students that entire year.

Educated lawyer

An investment counselor went out on her own. She was shrewd and diligent, so business kept coming in. Pretty soon she realized she needed an in-house counsel, so she began interviewing young lawyers.

"As I'm sure you can understand," she started off with one of the first applicants, "in a business like this, our personal integrity must be beyond question. Mr. Peterson, are you an honest lawyer?"

"Honest?" replied the job prospect. "Let me tell you about honest. Why, I'm so honest that my father lent me fifteen thousand dollars for my education, and I paid back every penny plus interest the minute after I tried my first case."

"Impressive! And what sort of case was that?"

The lawyer squirmed in his seat and admitted, "My father sued me for the outstanding debt."

Inflation

A little old lady sold pretzels on a street corner for twenty-five cents each. Every day a young lawyer would leave his office building at lunch-time and, as he passed her pretzel stand, he would leave her a quarter but would never take a pretzel.

This went on for more than five years. The two of them never spoke, but each day the two would make eye contact.

One day, as the lawyer passed the old lady's pretzel stand and left his quarter as usual, the pretzel woman spoke to him, "Sir, I appreciate your business. You are one of my best customers, but you need to know something. Our pretzel price has increased to thirty-five cents."

Sick-leave abuse

Negotiations between union members and their employer were at an impasse. The union denied that their workers were flagrantly abusing the sick-leave provisions set out by their contract. The next day at the bargaining table, the company's chief negotiator held aloft the morning newspaper, "This man," he announced as he pointed at the paper, "called in sick yesterday!"

There on the sports page was a photo of the supposedly ill employee who had just won a local golf tournament. Finally, the union negotiator broke the silence in the room. "Wow!" he said. "Just think—he might have broken the course record if he hadn't been sick!"

Cause and effect

A man applying for a job asked the interviewer whether the company would pay for his hospital insurance.

The interviewer said the worker would have to pay for it, but it was deducted from his check.

"The last place I worked the company paid for it," he said.

"Did they pay for your life insurance too?" asked the interviewer.

"Sure they did," the man said. "Not only that, but we got unlimited sick leave, severance pay, three weeks' vacation, a Christmas bonus, and coffee breaks."

"Then why did you leave such a perfect place?" the interviewer asked.

"They went bankrupt," the man admitted.

Thoughts

People say that hard work never killed anybody, but on the other hand, I've never known anybody who rested to death.

Wisdom

An angel appeared at a faculty meeting and told the dean that in return for his unselfish and exemplary behavior, the Lord would reward him with his choice of infinite wealth, wisdom, or beauty. Without hesitating, the dean selected infinite wisdom.

"Done!" said the angel and disappeared in a cloud of smoke and a bolt of lightning. Then all heads turned toward the dean who sat surrounded by a faint halo of light. He seemed stunned and shocked as a cloud of silence encompassed the room.

One of his colleagues leaned over and whispered to him, "Say something."

The dean, now filled with infinite wisdom said, "I should have taken the money."

Looking on the bright side

An applicant was seated in front of the human resources director. The director scanned the young applicant's résumé.

"I must say…you've been fired from every job you've held. There's not much positive in that!" said the director.

"Oh, I disagree, sir. At least I'm not a quitter!"

Good question

Charles was a moderately successful stockbroker who dreamed of making big money someday. He took his friend out for a drive, and he chose the route carefully in order to impress on him the possibilities of the brokerage business. They drove past huge houses and ended by the shore.

"Look at that yacht," he said as they drove slowly past a marina. "That '96 beauty belongs to the senior partner at Merrill Lynch. That one over there is owned by the head of Goldman and Sachs. And look at the huge one out there. That's the pride and joy of the top seller at Prudential-Bache."

His friend was silent. Charles turned to look at him and saw a pained look on his face.

"What's the matter?" Charles asked.

"I was just wondering," replied his friend. "Why aren't there any customers' yachts?"

Successful prescription

A regular customer at George's Gourmet Grocery marveled at the proprietor's quick wit and intelligence.

"Tell me, George, what makes you so smart?" he finally asked one day.

"I wouldn't share my secret with just anyone," George replied, lowering his voice so the other shoppers couldn't hear. "But since you're a good and faithful customer, I'll let you in on it—fish heads. You eat enough of them, and you'll be positively brilliant."

"You sell them here?" the customer asked.

"Sure, only $4 apiece," said George.

The customer bought three. A week later, he was back in the store complaining that the fish heads were disgusting and he wasn't any smarter.

"You didn't eat enough," said George. "You need to eat many more than that."

The customer went home with twenty more fish heads. Two weeks later, he was back, and this time he was really angry.

"Hey, George," he said, "you're selling me fish heads for $4 apiece when I just found out I can buy the whole fish for $2. You're ripping me off!"

"You see?" smiled George. "You're getting smarter already."

Two lawyers walked into the office one Monday morning, talking about their weekends. "I got a dog for my kids this weekend," said one.

The other attorney replied, "Good trade."

Defensive response

A young lad was watching the village blacksmith. The blacksmith began work, and the boy continued watching him shape a white-hot horseshoe. After the blacksmith finished, he threw the hot horseshoe over into the corner to cool.

The boy went over to pick it up, and the blacksmith warned him that it was still very hot.

The boy ignored the warning and picked up the horseshoe. He immediately dropped the horseshoe and began waving his hand in the air.

"Hot, wasn't it?" reminded the blacksmith.

Refusing to acknowledge his error, the boy replied, "Nope—it just doesn't take me long to look at a horseshoe."

Shorties

An executive was interviewing a nervous young woman for a position in his company. He wanted to find out something about her personality, so he asked, "If you could have a conversation with someone living or dead, who would it be?"

The girl quickly responded, "The living one."

A man got a note from his brother-in-law. He said his catering business was terrific. In fact, he said that he now had enough money to last him the rest of his life—as long as he died by next Tuesday.

Short and funny

Two male co-workers were eating lunch one day. One man said to his friend, "My wife talks to herself a lot."

His friend smiled and answered, "Mine does too, but she doesn't know it. She thinks I'm listening."

Ego time

A Hollywood producer called his friend, another Hollywood producer, on the telephone one evening.

"Hello," answered his friend.

"Hi, Tony," said the first producer. "This is Harold! How are you doing?"

"Great!" said his friend. "Listen to this! I just signed a multimillion-dollar deal with a major studio. I just sold a screenplay for over a million dollars to a hot new director. I have a new TV series that's coming on the air next month, and everyone says it's going to be a big hit. I'm doing great! How are you?"

"Fine," said the first producer. "Listen, Tony, I'll call you back when you're alone."

Quite a coincidence

A lawyer and an engineer were fishing in the Caribbean. The lawyer said, "I'm here because my house burned down, and everything I owned was destroyed by the fire. Fortunately, the insurance company paid for everything."

"That's quite a coincidence," said the engineer. "I'm here because my house and all my belongings were destroyed by a flood, and my insurance company paid for everything."

Puzzled, the lawyer asked, "How do you start a flood?"

Quickies

"I would like some vitamins for my son," the mother said as she walked into the pharmacy.

"Vitamin A, B, or C?" asked the pharmacist.

"It doesn't matter. He can't read yet."

Quick thinking

The shopkeeper was dismayed when a brand-new business much like his own opened up next door and erected a huge sign that read, "Best Deals." He was horrified when another competitor opened up on his right and announced its arrival with an even larger sign, "Lowest Prices."

The shopkeeper panicked, until he got an idea. He put the biggest sign of all over his own shop. It read, "Entrance."

Better reconsider

Two construction workers were working in the field on an extremely hot day. One pointed to the supervisor and said to the other, "Hey, how come we have to do all the work and he gets all the money?"

The other shrugged and said, "I don't know. Why don't you go over there and ask him."

So the first worker went up to the supervisor and said, "Hey, how come we do all the work and you get all the money?"

The supervisor answered, "Intelligence."

The worker asked, "What is this intelligence?"

The supervisor put his hand on a tree and said, "Hit my hand as hard as you can."

The worker wound up and with all his might tried to hit the supervisor's hand. Just as he almost did so, the supervisor pulled his hand away, and the worker hit the tree!

The supervisor explained, "That's intelligence."

Still hurting, the worker went back to his co-worker, who looked up and quietly asked, "Hey, what did he say?"

With a sheepish look on his face, the first worker puts his hand on his face and said, "Hit my hand as hard as you can."

Son-in-law

A very successful businessman had a meeting with his new son-in-law. "I love my daughter, and now I welcome you into the family by making you a 50-50 partner in my business. All you have to do is go to the factory every day and learn the operations."

The son-in-law responded, "I hate factories; I can't stand noise."

"I see," replied the man. "Well, then, you'll work in the office and take charge of the operations."

"I hate office work," said the son-in-law. "I can't stand being stuck behind a desk all day."

"Think a minute. I make you a half-owner of a successful business, and you turn down all positions. What am I going to do with you?"

"Easy," said the young man. "Buy me out."

The city slicker

A fellow owned a big ranch down in south Texas. His sister and her city-slicker husband came to visit. Trying to impress the city dude, the rancher took him to a large porch at the rear of the house. He pointed toward the horizon and said, "I can drive all day in that direction and never get to the property line."

"I know what you mean," replied the city slicker. "I used to have a car like that too."

More shorties

The blacksmith was instructing a novice in the way to treat a horseshoe. "I'll bring the shoe from the fire and lay it on the anvil. When I nod my head, you hit it with this hammer."

The apprentice did exactly as he was told, but he never hit a blacksmith again!

A woman walked up to the manager of a department store. "Are you hiring any help?" she asked.

"No," he said. "We already have all the staff we need."

"Then would you mind getting someone to wait on me?" she asked.

Thanks?

A motorist, after being bogged down in a muddy road, paid a farmer twenty dollars to pull him out with his tractor. He said to the farmer, "At those prices, I should think you'd be pulling people out of the mud day and night."

"Can't. At night I haul water for the hole."

A farmer was passing the insane asylum with a load of fertilizer. An inmate called through the fence, "What are you hauling?"

"Fertilizer," replied the farmer.

"What are you going to do with it?"

"Put it on my strawberries."

"And we put cream on ours, and they say we're crazy," the inmate countered.

Five cannibals were appointed as engineers in a defense company. During the welcoming ceremony the boss said, "You're all part of our team now. You can earn good money here, and you can go to the cafeteria for something to eat. So please don't trouble any of the other employees."

The cannibals promised. Four weeks later the boss returned and said, "You're all working very hard, and I'm very satisfied with all of you. However, one of our janitors has disappeared. Do any of you know what happened to him?"

The cannibals all shook their heads no. After the boss left, the leader of the cannibals said to the others, "Which of you nuts ate the janitor?"

A hand raised hesitantly, and the leader of the cannibals scolded, "You fool! For four weeks we've been eating team leaders, supervisors, and project managers, and no one noticed anything. And you have to go and eat the janitor!"

An employee went to the payroll department to complain that his check was ten dollars short.

"But our records show that you were overpaid ten dollars last week," the cashier responded, "and you didn't complain."

The worker replied, "An occasional mistake I can overlook, but not two in a row."

An applicant was filling out a job application. When he came to the question, "Have you ever been arrested?" he wrote, "No."

The next question, intended for people who had answered in the affirmative to the previous question, was, "Why?"

The applicant answered it anyway. "Never got caught."

SPORTSMANSHIP

The fisherman

One day a fisherman was lying on a beautiful beach with his fishing pole propped up in the sand and his solitary line cast out into the sparkling blue surf. He was enjoying the warmth of the afternoon sun and the prospect of catching a fish.

About that time, a businessman came walking down the beach, trying to relieve some of the stress of his workday. He noticed the fisherman sitting on the beach and decided to find out why this fisherman was fishing instead of working harder to make a living for himself and his family. "You aren't going to catch many fish that way," said the businessman. "You should be working rather than just lying on the beach!"

The fisherman looked up at the businessman, smiled, and replied, "And what will be my reward?"

"Well, you can get bigger nets and catch more fish!"

"And then what will be my reward?"

The businessman replied, "You will make money, and you'll be able to buy a boat, which will then result in larger catches of fish!"

"And then what will be my reward?" asked the fisherman.

"Then you can buy a bigger boat and hire some people to work for you!" the businessman answered in an exasperated tone.

"Then what will be my reward?" persisted the fisherman.

The businessman became angry. "Don't you understand? You can build up a fleet of fishing boats, sail all over the world, and let all your employees catch fish for you!"

Once again the fisherman asked, "And then what will be my reward?"

The businessman was red with rage when he shouted, "Don't you see that you can become so rich that you will never have to work again! You can spend all the rest of your days sitting on this beach, looking at the sunset. You won't have a care in the world!"

The fisherman, still smiling, said, "And what do you think I'm doing right now?"

Short stories

One day a Scotsman went playing golf. He asked the boy standing beside him, "You are the caddie for today?"

"Yes," answered the boy.

"You are good at finding lost balls?"

"Oh, yes, I find every lost ball!"

"OK, boy, then run and search for one. Then we can start!"

Smart thinking

Once there was a golfer whose drive landed on an anthill. Rather than move the ball, he decided to hit it where it lay. He gave a mighty swing. Clouds of dirt and sand and ants exploded from the spot—everything except the golf ball. It sat in the same spot. So he lined up and tried another shot. Clouds of dirt and sand and ants went flying again. The golf ball didn't even wiggle. Two ants survived. One dazed ant said, "Whoa! What are we going to do?"

Said the other ant, "I don't know about you, but I'm going to get on that ball!"

Cooperation

At one point during a baseball game, the coach said to one of his young players, "Do you understand what cooperation is? Do you understand what a team is?"

The little boy nodded in the affirmative.

"Do you understand that what matters is whether we win together as a team?" continued the coach.

Again the little boy nodded yes.

"So," persisted the coach, "when a strike is called, or you're out at first, you don't argue or curse or attack the umpire. Do you understand that?"

Once more the little boy nodded.

"Good," said the coach. "Now go over there and explain all that to your mother."

Modern technology

A husband and wife enjoyed taping programs on their VCR. They were known among their friends and family to be quite knowledgeable about taping. When their son and his expectant wife were visiting one day, the son asked, "Mom, if Sandy goes to the hospital on Super Bowl Sunday, would you tape it for me?"

Since his mother disliked football, she protested, "Me? Tape a game?"

"No, Mom," corrected the son. "The delivery."

Point of view

Some railroad laborers who had never seen golf were working near a course one morning. They were intrigued by the game and spent a lot of time watching the players. They saw a golfer knock the ball into a rut and have a hard time extracting it. Then he hit it into a sand trap and almost failed to get out.

Finally he had a good shot, and the ball trickled directly into the cup. Whereupon one of the workers who had watched the previous difficulties said sympathetically, "Now mister, you are really in trouble."

Golfing

A golfer hit his drive on the first hole three hundred yards right down the middle. When it came down, however, it hit a sprinkler and the ball went sideways into the woods.

He was angry, but he went into the woods and hit a very hard 2 iron, which hit a tree and bounced back straight at him. It hit him in the temple and killed him.

When he arrived at the Pearly Gates, St. Peter opened his big book, looked down the list, and said, "I see you were a golfer. Is that correct?"

"Yes, I was," he replied.

St. Peter said, "Do you hit the ball a long way?"

The golfer replied avidly, "You bet I do! After all, I got here in 2, didn't I?"

Super Bowl tickets

Bob won a ticket to the Super Bowl on a local radio station. On game day he loaded up the car, drove to the stadium, and found his seat, which—of course—was in the nosebleed section.

A couple of minutes into the first quarter, Bob was watching the game through his binoculars and noticed there was a man on the fifty-yard line—right next to an open seat. Every couple of plays, Bob checked, and the seat stayed vacant. Shortly before halftime, Bob decided that if the seat was still open at the beginning of the third quarter, he was going to try to claim it.

The seat stayed open, and Bob decided to go try it. He made his way down and asked the gentleman next to the seat if the seat was taken.

The man replied, "The seat was supposed to be for my wife. We haven't missed a Super Bowl in thirty years. Sadly, she just passed away."

Bob, embarrassed, said, "I'm very sorry to hear that. I'm sure it must be difficult coming to the Super Bowl alone for the first time in thirty years. But gosh, these are the two best seats in the stadium. Couldn't you find any friends or relatives to come to the game with you? After all, it is the Super Bowl!"

"No," the man replied. "They're all at the funeral."

Welcome to America

Jose had lived in San Juan all his life, and he had one desire—to see a baseball game in Yankee Stadium. He loved baseball; he loved the Yankees. So he worked and saved until he could afford an airplane ticket to New York during the baseball season.

He arrived in New York and made his way to Yankee Stadium, only to find the game sold out. His disappointment and story touched the manager's heart, and he agreed to let Jose sit way out in the bleachers behind the flagpole.

Upon returning to San Juan, all his friends were eager to hear about his grand adventure. "How was your trip? How was the game? How were the New Yorkers?" they all asked.

Jose raved—the trip was smooth, the game was fabulous, the New Yorkers were kind. "After they found a seat for me at the game, they all stood up and faced me to ask, 'Jose, can you see?'"

A groaner

A guy took his girlfriend to her first football game. Afterward he asked her how she liked the game.

"I liked it, but I could not understand why they were killing each other for twenty-five cents," she said.

"What are you talking about?" he asked.

"Well, everyone kept yelling to get the quarter back!"

Exercise helps pregnancy

The room was full of pregnant women and their partners, and the Lamaze class was in full swing. The instructor was teaching the women how to breathe properly, along with informing the men how to give the necessary assurances at this stage of the plan. Couples were practicing the technique all over the room.

The teacher then announced, "Ladies, exercise is good for you. Walking is especially beneficial. And, gentlemen, it wouldn't hurt you to take the time to go walking with your partner!"

The room really got quiet.

Finally, a man in the middle of the group raised his hand.

"Yes?" asked the teacher.

"Is it all right if she carries a golf bag while we walk?"

Golf or hole in one

The golfer stepped up to the tee and drove off. The ball sailed down the fairway, leaped onto the grass, and rolled into the hole. The golfer threw his club into the air with excitement.

"Have you suddenly gone crazy?" asked his wife, who was trying to learn the game.

"Why, I just did a hole in one!" yelled the golfer.

"Did you?" his wife asked placidly. "Do it again, dear. I didn't see you."

Fishing

A game warden noticed how a particular fellow named Sam consistently caught more fish than anyone else. When the other guys would only catch three or four a day, Sam would come in off the lake with a boat full.

The warden asked Sam his secret. The successful fisherman invited the game warden to accompany him and observe. So the next morning the two met at the dock and took off in Sam's boat.

When they got to the middle of the lake, Sam stopped the boat, and the warden sat back to see how it was done. Sam's approach was simple. He took out a stick of dynamite, lit it, and threw it in the air. The explosion rocked the lake with such a force that dead fish immediately began to surface. Sam took out a net and started scooping them up.

Well, you can imagine the reaction of the game warden. When he recovered from the shock of it all, he began yelling at Sam, "You can't do this! I'll put you in jail, buddy! You will be paying every fine there is in the book!"

Meanwhile, Sam set his net down and took out another stick of dynamite. He lit it and tossed it in the lap of the warden with these words: "Are you going to sit there all day complaining, or are you going to fish?"

Sometimes kids are better off left alone

Sandy eagerly began a job as an elementary school counselor. One day during recess she noticed a girl standing by herself on one side of a playing field while the rest of the kids enjoyed a game of soccer at the other end. Sandy approached and asked if she was all right. The girl said she was. A little while later, Sandy noticed the girl was in the same spot, still by herself. So Sandy offered, "Would you like me to be your friend?"

The girl hesitated, then said, "OK."

Feeling she was making progress, Sandy then asked, "Why are you standing here all alone?"

"Because," the little girl said with great exasperation, "I'm the goalie!"

A Russian track coach, interviewed by an American sportswriter, was asked why Soviets are now producing such fast runners.

"It's quite simple," the coach replied. "We use real bullets in our starting guns."

A local community club was organizing a baseball team. They could only muster eight players and were hard put to find a ninth. In desperation, they called on a new member, a very reserved Englishman who had just moved into the neighborhood from London, to join their team.

During the first game, the Englishman came to bat. On the very first pitch, he knocked the ball out of the park. The team members stood there, dumbfounded. Unfortunately, so did the Englishman. "Run!" his teammates cried. "Run!"

The Brit turned and stared at them icily. "I jolly well shan't run," he replied. "I'm perfectly willing to buy you chaps another ball."

Batter up

As I was driving home from work one day, I stopped to watch a local Little League baseball game that was being played in a park near my home. As I sat down behind the bench on the first base line, I asked one of the boys what the score was.

"We're behind 14 to nothing," he answered with a smile.

"Really?" I said. "I have to say, you don't look very discouraged."

"Why should we be discouraged? We haven't been up to bat yet!"

A man had been out playing golf. When he got home his neighbor asked him how he had done.

"I shot 70," the guy said.

"Hey, that's great," the neighbor replied.

The golfer said, "Yeah, I'll play the second hole tomorrow."

HOLIDAY FUN

A true story

I heard Jeff Smith, a.k.a. The Frugal Gourmet, read this letter from a viewer on the air: "I have had my turkey in the freezer for a year and a half. Will it take longer to thaw?"

Good answer

A lady was picking through the frozen turkeys at the grocery store, but she couldn't find one big enough for her family. She asked a stock boy, "Do these turkeys get any bigger?"

The stock boy replied, "No, ma'am, they're dead."

Last Thanksgiving, I had my chance to do the traditional thing of shooting my own turkey. Man, you should have seen the people scatter in the meat department.

Things to do at Thanksgiving

When everyone at the table takes turns saying what they are thankful for, say, "I'm thankful I didn't get caught," and refuse to say anything more.

Thanksgiving joke for the kids

Keep your eye off the turkey dressing. It makes him blush!

A Thought for Christmas

Do you know what would have happened if it had been three wise women instead of three wise men? They would have asked for directions, arrived on time, helped deliver the baby, cleaned the stable, made a casserole, brought practical gifts, and there would be peace on Earth.

OTHER BOOKS BY CHARLES AND FRANCES HUNTER

A Confession a Day Keeps the Devil Away
The Angel Book
Born Again! What Do You Mean?
Come Alive
Don't Be Afraid of Fear
Follow Me
God Is Fabulous
God's Answer to Fat...LOSE IT!
God's Big "IF"
God's Healing Promises
Revised Handbook for Healing
Hot Line to Heaven
How to Develop Your Faith
How to Find God's Will
How Do You Treat My Son, Jesus?
How to Heal the Sick
How to Make Your Marriage Exciting
How to Pick a Perfect Husband...or Wife
How to Receive and Maintain a Healing
How to Receive and Minister the Baptism With the Holy Spirit
Impossible Miracles
I Promise...Love, God
Let This Mind Be in You
Memorizing Made Easy
Shout the Word; Stop the Thief
Skinnie Minnie Recipe Book
Strength for Today
Supernatural Horizons
The Supernatural Spine
There Are Two Kinds of...
The Two Sides of a Coin
Watch Out! The Devil Wants Your Mind
What's in a Name

For more information on tapes, books, or other ministry opportunities, please write or call:

Charles and Frances Hunter Ministries

P. O. Box 5600

Kingwood, TX 77325-5600

(281) 358-7575

www.cfhunter.org